APPALACHIAN
REVIEW

VOL. 50, NO. 3
SUMMER 2022

TRADITION. DIVERSITY. CHANGE.

EDITOR
Jason Kyle Howard

BOOK REVIEWS EDITOR
Emily Masters

STUDENT ASSISTANTS
Lie Ford
Soul Nwaokoro
Ian Williamson

MANUSCRIPT READERS
Katherine Scott Crawford
Patti Frye Meredith

ADVISORY BOARD

Richard Hague
Marc Harshman
Maurice Manning
Karen Salyer McElmurray

Lee Smith
Lyrae Van Clief-Stefanon
Neela Vaswani
Crystal Wilkinson

ESTABLISHED IN 1973
PUBLISHED QUARTERLY
by Berea College
www.appalachianreview.net

Electronic submissions only at www.appalachianreview.net. Distributed through a partnership between the University of North Carolina Press and Duke University Press. Basic subscription price: $30/year for individuals, $60/year for institutions. For subscription requests and inquiries, visit the magazine's website, email subscriptions@dukepress.edu, or call 888-651-0122 (toll-free in the US and Canada) or 919-688-5134.

CONTENTS

COVER PHOTOGRAPH
Camping Trip by Kevin Schmid

EDITOR'S NOTE

In May, on the heels of a cold snap, Appalachian literature lost one of its finest poets with the death of Ron Houchin. I mention the chill in the air because when I think of Ron and his work, winter comes to mind—or at least a brisk day that calls for a thick, woolen cardigan to brave the elements. A grey Irish sky, dimming at the close of the day and speckled, perhaps, with a murmuration of starlings. Always, stillness. He had a way of suspending time in his poems—of directing his readers' vision with his own keen eyes and gift for language toward something worth witnessing, worth remembering.

As an editor, it was always a pleasure to publish his writing. I knew that whenever I opened one of his submissions I was in for an encounter that would see his words ring through my head the rest of the day. I will miss those emails, and I know our readers will miss his work.

In this issue, we are proud to announce the winners of the 2021 Denny C. Plattner Awards. Our fiction section features "Eviction Notice," a layered short story from Kasia Merrill, and we have the pleasure of introducing you to Leo Coffey, a promising young writer who contributes "Orange Soda." In her essay "Where Do You Come From," Rachel Kesselman takes the reader from Appalachian Pennsylvania to Paris and then to Washington, D.C. Quincy Gray McMichael, a nonfiction writer and poet who runs a farm in West Virginia, offers an evocative reflection on how the music of Paul Simon has carried her through life. Award-winning poet Kathleen Driskell transports us to other places and realms, and pays a moving tribute to her friend Claudia Emerson, the late Pulitzer Prize-winning poet, while Bill King contributes resonant poems steeped in the natural world. We're also proud to feature an interview with Neema Avashia, author of the much buzzed-about memoir *Another Appalachia: Coming Up Queer and Indian in a Mountain Place,* and an insightful craft essay on the work of Toni Morrison by Daniel Kennedy.

As autumn begins its approach, I'm reminded of one of Ron's poems, "Unrequited Everything," of his absence—and his continued presence:

> *The day hugged emptiness, the familial*
> *sound of raw rain, a close echo of metal*
> *and sighs. No sun distracted from the mystery*
> *of coming darkness. A name*
> *hung like an answered prayer.* ∎

2021 DENNY C. PLATTNER AWARDS

The annual Plattner Awards were established in 1995 by Kenneth and Elissa Plattner to honor their late son and his love of writing. The awards are given to the finest pieces of fiction, creative nonfiction, and poetry that appeared in *Appalachian Review* during the previous year. Winners receive a $200 prize, and both winners and honorable mentions are awarded a handsome piece of handmade ceramics designed and manufactured by Berea College Crafts.

FICTION
Judged by Monic Ductan, author of the forthcoming
Daughters of Muscadine: Stories

Winner: Laura Demers, "Clinch River Ashes"
Honorable Mention: Monica Brashears, "The Trouble With Snakes"

CREATIVE NONFICTION
Judged by Patricia L. Hudson, author of Traces: A Novel

Winner: Elaine Neil Orr, "Old Woman at My Window"
Honorable Mention: William Kelley Woolfitt, "A Is for Ark Population"

POETRY
Judged by Jayne Moore Waldrop author of
Drowned Town, Pandemic Lent: A Season in Poetry, *and* Retracing My Steps

Winner: Matthew Hawk, "Drive-In Movie During a Pandemic"
Honorable Mentions: Laura Neal, "In Sickness" and Despy Boutris, "Moonless Pastoral"

EVICTION
NOTICE

KASIA MERRILL

It's not personal, it's business.

That's what I always said. It sounded different coming out of someone else's mouth. Jerry had a hold of one end of my couch, Liam had the other. Only it wouldn't fit through the goddamn door. Nothing ever fit through that door. We had to get the couch in through the window. Not that I was going to tell them that.

Jerry's face was ripe and sweaty, the black scrub of his beard glistening with sweat. "Jesus, how'd you get this in here?"

I had moved a lot of places. Moving was like Tetris. I was good at Tetris when I was a kid, and I was just as good at hauling furniture. It wasn't ever my intention to get into evictions, but that was where the money was. Not much money, but enough to scrape by. Only life wasn't like Tetris. Life was like Snake where your debts kept getting bigger and bigger until you ran into yourself, and *bam*, there was the red paper slapped on the door and your stuff carried out on the street by some other family man shmuck who thinks he's still got it alright because the head of the snake hasn't hit him yet.

I watched Jerry from the bottom stair, didn't say anything. I was at his daughter's wedding. We'd shared a bottle of beer. There weren't many men I could say that about.

The green couch was becoming white at the bottom from all the shoving. The door frame groaned under its push. It wasn't going further.

It got me thinking about when Helen went into labor. All that shoving, that groaning, the crown of our daughter's head. Elsie, we called her. I'd never felt so helpless, watching Helen's face pinch and flush with a long scream. Only thing I could do was watch. Say *Good job, baby, you got this.* It didn't matter what I said. There was nothing I could do and I had to watch someone else's pain give me the thing I wanted.

I felt the same there. Helpless. Watching that couch that cost me an $800 down payment be shoved through the door of a house I couldn't afford. And what could I do? Just watch from the stairs. I was the helpless one.

Evan walked in from the living room, his young wrestler's shoulders strapped into a shoulder dolly. He leaned on the doorframe, one white headphone shoved into the thick folds of his ear. "News says there's a tornado coming," he said, crossing his arms. He cracked a piece of gum between his teeth.

Jerry and me flicked our eyes towards him. He was a new kid, hadn't moved as many houses as us, always had those damn earbuds shoved into his head. Last week, we'd moved an old couple from a rowhouse down on Bernard's, and he'd shattered the lady's vase when he tossed a box into the yard, hadn't even had the decency to remove that damn earbud to hear her crying.

"It'll clear," Jerry said. "Bank says everything's gotta be out by tomorrow."

Upstairs, I could hear Tony and Mic dissembling the bed. Helen told me I should be the one to dissemble it, make sure it stayed in good condition, but I told her I wasn't lifting a finger to do anything that made their job easier.

"They're your co-workers," Helen said. "You're going to have to see them next Monday."

"They'll be my co-workers on Monday, but they're my evictors 'til then," I said.

Helen just shook her head at me. I knew what she was thinking. I was being stubborn for no good reason. I was thinking the same thing, but it didn't stop me from sitting on the stair with my arms crossed.

Jerry stopped shoving at the couch. I could hear Liam on the other side, only his wrinkled forehead visible. "We takin' a break?"

Jerry wiped at his face, stepped towards me. I thought of the time we were hired to move an old drunk from his childhood home, how he'd swung at me when I accidentally knocked over a picture frame from the wall. Jerry had been the first to step up, hit the guy squarely in the face, then brought some ice over afterwards.

That was the job. You hit, you iced. You knew you could be one of the poor losers you were moving at any moment because you were also hanging on by a thread. You knew you, too, could one day be watching everything that meant something look dumb and meaningless in someone else's hands, tossed into the dirt.

You knew it, but still, some part of you just didn't expect it. It was the difference between the tornado warning and seeing the cloud firsthand.

I set the beer beside me and stood. My back felt like one of those neon bracelets Elsie liked to wear, like I could crack it and it'd explode in an unflinching light.

"You have to use the window," I said.

Jerry clapped his hand on my shoulder. "There's our man," he said.

"And watch the goddamn couch," I said. "You're tearing it to shit."

■ ■ ■

We'd bought the house after Elsie was born.

Nothing special, nothing big. Two floors, two bedrooms. A smear of a living room, a fleck of a kitchen. Helen liked it, said it was cozy, tacked our pictures on the walls and placed succulents on the windowsills. Said they brought life into the house. Only thing was she kept almost killing them, but I never had the heart to tell her she wasn't a nurturer. I had to sneak into the living room while she elevated her swollen nurse ankles in our bed and tend those prickled sticks back to life. Helen must've known someone was helping keep her plants alive, but if she did, she never said anything.

The house wasn't much of a home until Elsie came. She was an ugly thing, pink and writhing like an earthworm carried in from the garden. Everyone kept calling her a miracle because Helen was almost forty years old, but the real miracle was how much I loved that girl, how the minute she'd tucked my finger into her palm, she'd staked a claim in me like a flag in a foreign land she'd found.

No one ever told me that about kids, how fucked up it is to love them. How you can think up a million different ways they could die or hurt themselves. How every cough and every scrape ruins you on a deeper and deeper level until you become excavated of the person you used to be.

After Jerry got the couch through the window, he walked up with me to Elsie's room. The other guys followed; Liam and Evan still yapping away about the tornado warning. "We gotta get him out of here by tonight," Jerry repeated over his shoulder. We walked upstairs in an assembly line.

I picked up Barry, Elsie's teddy, and realized I'd made a mistake. It should have been Helen's soft hands to hold it, not Evan's fighter fists.

Helen had already packed most of the room the night before, but I told her she could quit, that we weren't trying to make anyone's job easier. I picked up Barry, Elsie's teddy, and realized I'd made a mistake. It should have been Helen's soft hands to hold it, not Evan's fighter fists.

Jerry took one look at my face, then told the guys to go grab some beers from the fridge downstairs. He started picking up the toys and placing them in the boxes, holding them like they were newborn kittens. I didn't have to say anything to him to let him know how thankful I was. I leaned against the doorframe.

"Got a job up in Harvey tomorrow. You're lucky to miss out on that one," he said.

"How big?"

"Four-bedroom."

"That's nothing. Liam tell you we had a six-bedroom last weekend?"

Jerry whistled, dropped Sophie the giraffe into the pile of stuffed animals. "Big family?"

"Just a couple. Fucking people, man. Buying things they can't afford. They had a pool, too. Greedy." I pulled on the beer in my hand. "Buying things *we* can't afford," I added.

"Well, this house we're doing tomorrow," Jerry pressed down into his good leg to stand. His knee cracked. He scratched at his beard. "Rob says the guy's a hoarder. City official warned him, man. That's how bad it is. Guess how many cats."

"Ten."

"Thirty at least."

"You're kidding me."

Jerry shook his head, sealed up the box. He limped over to the dresser. "This ready?"

■ ■ ■

When I got outside, I was surprised to see Helen heaving boxes into our rust-flecked SUV. Her legs were thick straps in her cut-off jeans, molded from twelve-hour nursing shifts down at the hospital. Elsie was shooting across the yard like a firecracker someone lit off.

Helen smiled at me like we were packing for vacation, like she thought we were in a different story than we really were, but I could see in the faded lines of her cheek that she was putting on a show, just pretending, like she did at the hospital with her patients when she had to be the thin veil between reality and hope.

"Thought I'd pack these valuables myself before these oafs drop all my nana's china," she said. She winked at me, rolled her eyes at the guys. They laughed in response and I loved Helen for making them do that, for being a piece of my life that nobody could toss out into my lawn without regretting it, without knowing that they were tossing something precious.

The yard already looked like a graveyard, like an upended life, but it was better than the usual evictions. Nobody had strewn my clothes across the grass, left my TV on the curb. Everything was neat, organized, treated with care. Jerry had said more to the guys than I'd thought.

Elsie the rocket ricocheted into my arms. "Daddy, why's our stuff outside?" she asked. Her dark curls, taken straight from her mother, cascaded out of her ponytail, but her eyes were mine through and through.

"Remember how we told you we're moving in with Gram and Gramps?" I asked her. She nodded. "This is how we do it."

She considered this, then smiled. "Daddy, I got something to show you." She looped her fingers together, taking an extra moment of concentration to get her index fingers to touch. Those little fingers, so clumsy and uncoordinated. Sometimes I found myself counting them when she fell asleep in my arms, confirming she was whole. Perfect. "Here is the church—"

"Here is the steeple," I said.

She huffed. "Daddy, don't say it. I'm saying it."

"There's supposed to be a tornado coming," Helen called from the car. "We heard it on the news." Helen stood, brushed off her bare legs. "We better hurry."

Elsie's wide gaze turned toward me for confirmation. "There's no tornado," I said, holding Elsie's head in my palm and picking dried jam off her cheek. She shoved my hands away. I never expected being a dad would've made me a liar, but there were just some things in the world that weren't right to say.

"Thanks, Mr. Weatherman," Helen responded, taking a bundle of wrapped dresses from Liam's arms, hooking them into the backseat of our car.

Elsie lifted her head like she'd caught the scent of something. I looked up to see Evan toss a box of her toys into the front yard with his eyes glazed over, lost in whatever was playing on those damn earbuds, and I had half a mind to yank them out and smash them. The box tumbled over, spilling Elsie's prized possessions: a jar of pinecones she'd saved from her nana's house, a few dog-eared Dr. Seuss books, a white bunny gone brown from spit and tears.

She wiggled from my arms, mouth already broken open in a cry. "Those are mine!" she shouted, stomping her feet as she crossed the yard.

I expected Helen to do something. She knew what to do in these situations, shit if I did. I'd never spent much time around kids before having one of my own—Helen, now she used to babysit, work with kids in the hospital. But she didn't do anything. She just stood there, same as me, gaping at her daughter, a box framed in her hands, her pretend smile now swallowed into the strain of her cheeks, the wetness of her eyes.

Evan was already heading back into the house, but our little firecracker took off after him while me and Helen were too useless to react, gave him a good swift kick in the back of his leg like she did when we played soccer and she wanted the ball. I hoped it hurt, but I knew from experience there wasn't much punch behind it. Evan looked down at her, oblivious to the pain she was hellbent on giving him, and tousled her hair before heading back inside. Didn't he know to drop to his leg, feign pain? Let her have the power of hearing *ow* in response to her fury? She stood in the yard, hands balled into fists, shoulders trembling.

"Those are my toys," she said after him, voice caked in snot.

"She shouldn't be here to see this," I said. "Why didn't you leave her with your parents?"

Helen shrugged, wiped her eyes against her shoulder. "There was a tornado warning," she said. "I wanted her with us."

■ ■ ■

Elsie took a popsicle and fifteen minutes of YouTube to calm down, then fell into a sticky daze in her car-seat among the tower of boxes in the back of Helen's hatchback. I sat with her for a couple minutes before her eyes sealed shut, told her everything would be fine. Her eyes were glued to Helen's phone, cheeks streaked with dirty tears and cherry slush.

Helen had repacked the box with Elsie's things in it, promised her it'd rest in the front seat of my pickup. Told her we'd make sure to keep it safe.

"What if a tornado comes?" she asked.

"We'll bring it down into the cellar with us," we said.

My stomach turned into knots at what she might say next; *we don't have a cellar anymore.* But she didn't say it because she was our kid and she trusted us, trusted us to know better and provide for her, even at the moment when we were failing, when our shit was strewn across the yard, being marched like ants into the unknown of our future. Helen and I had made plans to stay with her parents, but I didn't like to think about it too much. About the basement we'd be sleeping in, about the temporariness of our lives.

We'd tried a hundred different ways to move money around, make it work, but somehow it just kept dipping down until there was a bigger hole, until the green grass we were trying to dig our way back up to was no longer in sight. And it was just debt. Deep, deep debt; the dirt covering our graves.

By the time Elsie was asleep, the sky had darkened into a moldy green. Helen kept glancing at it. She hurried back into the house, re-emerged, arms loaded with boxes, expression salty. I pulled another beer from the tinkling ice of the cooler, leaving my hand just a minute longer so it could go numb. Jerry walked out carrying the headboard of our bed, glanced up at the sky, shook his head.

"We better get a move on," he said.

■ ■ ■

The first time I did an eviction, I wasn't much older than Evan. Helen and I had just gotten married, wanted to buy a house, and I didn't have a whole lot of options. I wasn't good in offices—got too stir-crazy. The construction company I'd worked for was stocked full of people I didn't much care for. Jerry was a friend of my uncle's from the Marines and hired me on the spot.

The first move was Maria Perry, a woman I used to know in high school. She was two grades above me and used to buy me beer when I didn't have an ID. She was sitting on the front steps when we got there, wearing hiking boots and a silk robe, her dark hair pulled back in a loose ponytail. I ducked my head, didn't look her in the eye, hoping she wouldn't recognize me.

Her landlord hired us to evict her, and he followed us through the rooms, barking orders. He was a hopped-up guy with a beer belly and thin blonde hair that crawled like a spider from his ears. Maria stayed on the porch the whole time, lighting cigarettes and filling a coffee cup with Smirnoff. The neighborhood kids cruised their bikes up and down the block, straining to see who it was getting the boot this week. I was curious how she'd aged—I'd always liked her back when we were kids—but I didn't want to look too long in case she'd recognize me.

I didn't have any choice when I found the cat, crunched into a hiding spot beneath her bedframe. It was old with matted fur chalky with dust. It howled when I picked it up, went silent when I pulled it close. "Check out how the newbie handles pussy," Liam joked as I walked down the stairs. I ignored him.

Maria was out in the yard when I came out, walking slowly with a cigarette between her lips, picking clothes from the grass with the hook of her fingers.

"Forget someone?" I said.

She glanced up, straightened her back. "Shit," she said. She opened her arms and waved her hands. "Give me, give me."

I transferred the cat into her hooked arms, keeping my gaze down. She pulled her cat tight into her body, inhaled its dusty head. "Thanks."

I figured we'd laugh it off, that she'd say thanks for her cat, thanks for taking care, but she looked up at me then, eyes cold as December frost.

"Yep."

"I remember you, you know," she said. I figured we'd laugh it off, that she'd say thanks for her cat, thanks for taking care, but she looked up at me then, eyes cold as December frost. "See what I get for being nice to you in high school, you heartless fuck."

Her cat stared at me from over her shoulder as she carried it to her car, its eyes moving in a slow stupid blink. I headed back into her bedroom, empty except for one last box, which I gave a swift kick. I don't know why she got to me so much, but I didn't like her thinking I was a bad person. It bothered me more than it usually did. I'd done shit before—busted up a guy so bad he ended up in the hospital—but I'd never cared much before.

After we finished the job, Jerry and Liam took me to get beers to celebrate my first move. We did a round of Jameson on Jerry, shot a game of pool. Just before we left, Jerry wiped his moustache with his handkerchief, tucked it in his pocket, said, "Remember, kid. Job is to move them out, not get stuck in there with them. Don't take nothing home with you."

■ ■ ■

People think the telltale sign of tornadoes are rain and stormy weather, but that isn't true. That's hurricanes. The telltale sign of a tornado is when the air gets real still, so still you almost feel dizzy. It's like you can smell it picking up, like at the beginning of a long night of adventures, when you know you're about to do something stupid. That heavy pause.

I knew the tornado was coming as soon as I stepped outside holding half the dining table. "Fuck, we need to get out of here," Jerry said from behind me.

The sky was molded with clouds and I was suddenly worried, worried about where we'd stick our stuff now that we were out of the house that'd held us tight three years ago when a tornado blazed through and tore up the playground down the street. Helen's mother's house had a cellar, but a rickety one, not the kind I trusted. Jerry and I hustled across the lawn, Evan coming out right behind us to announce he was heading home.

"Like hell you are," Jerry said. "You leave when we all leave."

"You boys get on out of here," Helen called through the upstairs window. "Me and Ray will handle the rest."

"What are we going to do with our stuff?" I yelled back, but she was already gone, or else she was pretending she couldn't hear me. Jerry and I heaved the table onto the moving van, while Evan pealed out of the driveway and down the street in his pickup, his smokestacks billowing clouds behind him. I was glad to see him gone.

"You sure you got this?" Jerry asked, eyeing the various boxes still stacked around the yard. "Maybe we stick around for a few more minutes, make sure everything's in." He swatted at a mosquito on the back of his neck. "Just remember, the house is supposed to be cleared out by tonight."

"Yeah, yeah, I know the drill. You and the boys get the last boxes out, I'm gonna check on Els." I stooped down to grab one of Elsie's yellow plastic dump trucks and toss it in the pile of garbage drooling from the mouth of the trashcan. Shit I don't remember buying or needing or wanting, but there it was, stacked one on top of the other, mattering close to nothing when there was nowhere to keep them.

I thought of Elsie's pleading eyes, "Daddy, I *need* this. Why does Katie get one but I don't?" and I never had an answer for that question, no parent did, and so home we went with Elsie's lap full of toys, home to Helen shaking her head and reminding me of the stacks of red bills waiting on my workbench. As if I forgot.

We'd have to give up one of the cars, but Helen and I couldn't agree on which one. She hated my truck, and stubborn ass that she was, refused to drive stick, but I needed a truck for moving. I couldn't see myself cruising around to moving jobs in a hatchback, or even worse, getting dropped off by Helen like a kid at preschool. Liam would get a kick out of that, seeing Helen waving me off and handing me my lunchbox.

I sighed as I approached the hatchback. Helen would win. She always won. "With you, I've got the spine of a sea sponge," I once complained.

I rubbed my eyes, thinking what to tell Elsie to not get her too worked up or scared about hiding in the cellar, but when I looked in the car, she wasn't there. I yanked open the door, searched through the back seat, wrenching out Helen's carefully packed boxes and throwing them onto the sidewalk. The wind picked up, caught a stack of Helen's dresses and dragged them in the dirt. I grabbed them in a bundle, shoved them back in, and tore off towards my truck sitting in the driveway.

A light rain flecked from the sky. Helen opened the window, told me to get Elsie, and I told her, "Yeah, yeah, I will, give me a minute."

"What's wrong?"

My truck was full of suitcases and bags, but empty of what I wanted, what I needed. The box of Elsie's toys that we promised to keep were pulled out onto the floor beneath the steering wheel, objects thrown out across the truck bed. The work of little hands. I went through the items. Dr. Seuss books, the white bunny, but the jar of pinecones was missing. I turned around. Helen was standing on the front step, palms pressed together like she was already praying against what I had to say, pointer fingers pushed together at the tip of her lips. *Open the doors and see all the people.*

"I can't find Elsie," I said.

■ ■ ■

Before I met Helen, I used to drive just to get lost. I never wanted to go anywhere special, just wanted to not know where I was for a moment, for a second, for an hour. A day. Once I got so lost I ended up in a different state, spent the night curled up in my car by a cornfield. I found some old hippie hitchhiking down the road and we stopped at a roadhouse with no sign, lost ourselves to the night with conversation and liquor that made our brains sweet.

I don't look to get lost like that much anymore. Maybe because I grew old, or maybe because with old age, I feel more lost than ever. As a kid, I used to think getting old meant things would get under your control, but it's the opposite.

"Elsie!" Helen screamed beside me, her sneakers slapping against the blacktop. The sky bruised with fury.

"Elsie!" My voice thundered behind hers, wild like a chased animal.

Elsie was too young to remember the last tornado, about three years back. Helen and I took her little sleeping body downstairs, holed up against the water heater and cracked open a bottle of whisky as our girl dozed in the nook of Helen's arm. We'd made fun of it, but only because we were scared. Me and Helen were the same when we met each other. Neither of us had anything to lose. She liked getting lost with me, and we'd drive until we ran out of gas, then take off running in a random direction. Once we ended up in some pissed-off farmer's field, laughing as he shot at the ground to scare us.

"Elsie!" Jerry shouted from two blocks down the other direction.

I screamed her name until my voice went hoarse, until Helen wrapped her hand around my forearm and said "Ray" in a tone that prickled my skin.

We'd reached the end of the block where the horizon was visible beyond the green stretch of the baseball field. I'd told Elsie I'd teach her to make those bleachers go crazy, and not with some cheap dance like she'd spotted the older girls doing, but by cracking balls against her bat, by racing over bases.

Across the field on the horizon, the sky had pinched into one blackened finger, reaching from the sky to claw the ground. It had to be miles away from where we were standing, but it didn't make it look less intimidating, and when I glanced over, Helen was walking in a trance back to the house, lip quivering.

When she got stressed, she got silent, which meant I needed to do the talking, so I started telling her about the field, about what I'd told Elsie, like our biggest problem was prepping our little girl for baseball season. Helen nodded and I kept talking because if I didn't, I wasn't sure what would seep in to fill the silence.

We had just started walking back towards the house when there she was, as miraculous as when she was first born, standing tall and brave at the bottom of the aluminum slide, holding her jar of pinecones to her chest. She wasn't scared or crying, but her expression changed when she saw us barreling towards her.

Across the field on the horizon, the sky had pinched into one blackened finger, reaching from the sky to claw the ground.

"You can't just walk off like that," Helen said, dragging Elsie into her chest, talking into the top of her head.

She held up her jar of pinecones. "I wanted to get a pinecone from the playground before the tornado ran it down," she said.

A part of me felt furious. Furious for the panic she set ablaze in my chest, unregistered to her little blinking eyes. I grabbed the jar right out of her hands and lifted it up, wanting her to understand how she made me feel, wanting her to be as upset. My pulse hammered the palms of my hands. Helen stared at me, her eyes saying more than she needed to, as Elsie jumped out of her arms in a fuss, alarmed that for once, I was about to take something of hers, and maybe that was good, maybe she needed to feel that for a change.

She stilled, lifted a hand to point behind me. "What's that?" she asked, seeing the funnel cloud for the first time. She wrapped her arms around her mother, pressed her cheek into her thigh. "I want to go home."

What home?

"I'll carry these for you," I said. "I'll keep them safe." I tapped the pinecone jar with my fingernail. Elsie nodded, trusting me. Maybe she had no other choice, but I like to think she did. ■

BLUE COLLAR TO MIDDLE CLASS

My parents aspired to climb into the middle
class and cling tight. PTA, golf scrambles,
Bridge. A frothy whiskey sour, plastic pink
spear, complete with hilt, driven through
the bright maraschino cherry and an orange
slice dropped atop and floating in chipped
ice, ordered whenever out with couples
who had learned to ask for their steaks
medium rare, sneering at the sweet French
dressing the waitress rattled off with options
for tossed salads. Instead, they requested
creamy Italian, just then in vogue.

The wives pulled the cherry stems through
their teeth and shook their heads. No,
of course, they won't allow their children
to be bussed—though, they did not think
of themselves as bigots. Hadn't they just come
of age in the Age of Aquarius? Hadn't they
rolled up the carpets in their living rooms,
pushed them against the walls, and allowed
Chubby Checker to teach them how to twist?

KATHLEEN DRISKELL

TIARA

As the Homecoming King escorted Brenda
across our football field, all heads, in unison,
turned from looking at her to Mr. Rausch,
our biology teacher, who sat with his wife
in the bleachers, his two little kids merrily
throwing popcorn at each other, laughing
and swinging their feet wildly.

Mrs. Rausch was so dour looking, so rumpled,
her hairdo a frizzy salon-frosted wedge,
that I'm sure most thought *well no wonder*
as we compared her to the beaming Miss
Oldham County Homecoming 1976. There
were insects whining in the halo of
the field's floodlights, but Brenda, her tiara,
her blue sateen gown with its princess
neckline, twinkled sweetly down below.

KATHLEEN DRISKELL

JEWISH CEMETERY, PRAGUE

I learned when I visited
the Jewish cemetery in Prague,
that the dead were relegated
to one plot behind their synagogue,
so small that layering graves became
the only way to give way for the new

dead; consequently, in that graveyard
the ground provides no mossy idyll.
All appears to be erupting, the headstones,
wrecked teeth, as if dead are struggling
to escape their coffins, as if the dead
have learned that for some
there is no place to be forgotten.

KATHLEEN DRISKELL

RIVER WALK IN WINTER

For Claudia Emerson

All is quiet here this morning.
It's too cold and early for runners,
though their kids are already
in yellow buses on the roads over there
beyond these woods.

No one is walking a dog,
yet, despite the wind, most
dogs would be here happily.

In the year or so before she died,
when able, she'd walk in a park
along a path next to a river,
somewhat like this,
and try not to think about cells
dividing. And growing. So odd
to think of growing as a negative.
Especially now. In winter, I mean.

She was loved again.

And, she loved him.

She loved dogs, too, but she grew
so angry, she said (she needn't have,
I heard the rage in her voice),
when they came bounding toward
her off their leashes, their owners
walking casually behind,

expecting everyone to be
as delighted as they
that they owned
such marvelous creatures.

I feel compelled to defend her,
to say again that she loved dogs.

To make sure that you heard me.

She loved all animals, really.

(She loved the whole fucking world.)

So maybe it was as those dogs
bounded toward her, they made her realize
just how easily, then, she could be completely
knocked off her feet
by what she loved.

KATHLEEN DRISKELL

PSALM FOR THE HERETIC

The lord is my shepherd and leads me
to slaughter. Let's not pretend
otherwise. After all, my mind
is frilled with tomorrows.
Why ask me to love the lamb
seized for your Sunday supper?
Oh, god, grant me a calendar
blank as a sheep's.

KATHLEEN DRISKELL

GRASPING
AT GRACE

QUINCY GRAY McMICHAEL

When I open the door of my father's truck, all I smell is hot banana. His Ford stays ripe with carpentry odors—sweat, sawdust—but he always has at least one brown banana on the dash, roasting in the Maine sun. I hold my breath as I scoot into the middle of the bench seat, arranging the belt across my lap, pretending to buckle my nine-year-old frame into the narrow center spot. My little brother Owen, still short and chubby at seven, steps onto the truck's diamond-plate running board, grasps hold of the armrest, and hauls himself inside.

My lungs beg for fresh air. "Dad, can you open the window?" I croak.

My father—whom I call Choad, like his friends do—complies, cranking the window open with his left hand while roaring the engine to life with his right. The cassette in the tape deck clicks into gear, flooding the cab with bewitching syncopation, over which Paul Simon sings: "The poor boy changes clothes and puts on aftershave, to compensate for his ordinary shoes." Owen leans over, red-faced and triumphant after his ascent to the favored seat by the window, and yanks the heavy door toward him to latch.

Before Simon can mention those diamond-studded soles, Choad is already harmonizing, slipping into an *ooo-ooo-ooo* falsetto alongside Simon for the chorus. As Choad croons, he buckles his seatbelt and looks over at us, his two unintentionally itinerant children, giving a quick glance to be sure we are belted and ready. He smiles his pumpkin grin and gives a little shake of the shoulders to signal that he is slipping into full vehicular boogie, with his flying fingers making a drum set of the dashboard and his rich voice catching every dip and flip of Simon's lyric rhythm. If the romantic incongruity in this song reminds Choad of my mother—or of that glorious lost monstrosity of a home built with his sweat and her money—he is hiding his pain like a master.

I am too young to match the rich girl and the poor boy in Simon's song with the complicated landscape of wealth and want that fractured my own parents' love, and our original family. Instead, I pray for a breeze to cut the thick aroma of banana as I squeeze my knees tight to the right to avoid the gearshift. Choad breaks his percussive rhythm just long enough to nudge the truck into first and we begin to roll.

■ ■ ■

Graceland is music for the road. Released just a year after my birth, Paul Simon's 1986 album, more than any other, has carried me from place to place. The title song urges the listener to get moving: even before the sincerity of Simon's vocals spill onto the track, the rolling drumbeat doubles as wheels on pavement, conjures the urgent rotation of guardrail spokes spinning past the window. In a recording created for the twenty-fifth anniversary edition of *Graceland*, Simon acknowledged this, saying: "The drums were something like— kind of a traveling rhythm in country music; I'm a big Sun Records fan, and early-'50s, mid-'50s Sun Records you hear that drum beat a lot, like a fast, Johnny Cash-type of rhythm." *Rolling Stone* credited Simon with crafting "a finely wrought personal reflection on lost love." *Graceland* soon became the soundtrack of my life.

Paul Simon's songwriting skill is no secret. *Rolling Stone* ranks him at number eight on their "100 Greatest Songwriters of All Time" list. I would probably inch him up a few notches, given Simon's ability to build the bones of a rich story in such few words while weaving "wit and literary detail" into the seamless telling. As he expressed to *Village Voice* contributor Robert Christgau: "I'm a relationship writer, relationships and introspection." Nowhere is this more apparent than on *Graceland*, and in the song "Graceland" itself.

In this song, Simon shares from the perspective of an undeniably imperfect, road-worn narrator who hauls his nine-year-old along with him, heartened by the hope that he—that they—will find life's answers in Elvis's hallowed Memphis home. Of "Graceland," commonly understood to be Simon's favorite song, not only from the album of the same name but of his sixty-plus-year career, the songwriter notes:

"The track has a beautiful emptiness to it." The song also exemplifies Simon's hallmark mix of deeply sincere storytelling and emotive, lively language. On the album *Graceland*—which is notable both in its prominence within the musical canon and as a point of transition in Simon's career—the songwriter broadens the tradition of collaborative creation for which he was already known.

The early 1980s were hard on Simon. Two key relationships had disintegrated: his marriage to Carrie Fisher and his partnership with longtime collaborator Art Garfunkel. Simon's 1983 album *Hearts and Bones* fared poorly on the musical charts. He had just crested forty, and his son Harper, then his only child, was entering adolescence. After listening to a bootleg tape of South African mbaqanga—'township jive'—Simon found his way to Johannesburg, where the peerless poetry of *Graceland* was born.

In addition to the many musicians with whom Simon recorded on that trip—including isicathamiya *a cappella* vocalists—*Graceland* carries forth the voices of Louisiana Zydeco, Mexican-American music, and Simon's traditional rock-pop amalgam. "That's really the secret of World Music, is people are able to listen to each other and make associations, and play their own music that sounds like it fits into another culture," Simon has said. This interplay is apparent across *Graceland*'s landscape, and the resultant complexity proves the album timeless. The music of *Graceland* has traveled across the decades with me.

■ ■ ■

As our bus wound through towering rocks in hues from ruddy to ochre, my partner Richard and I started to notice shiny hatchbacks and dusty vans crowding the narrow road shoulders. Soon, the trickle of Colorado concertgoers hiking beside the vehicles became a flood, spilling into stuffed parking lots, which appeared to have been carved from the jutting earth.

We stepped off the bus wearing sunglasses, yet still squinting and shading our eyes against the westerly setting sun. "I guess it's this way," suggested Richard, and we joined the herd, tramping the near half-mile from the lower parking area, snaking past those who stopped to rest, along the paved path—up, up, and around until the carved-rock ampitheatre came into focus. Then, up, up, up some more—looking for our row, jostling and laughing with the rest of the eager, aging crowd. Our common effort seemed to create a special kind of camaraderie: once we found our seats, we looked around to realize that every person in attendance had committed sweat equity to our shared experience that night.

Soon, the trickle of Colorado concertgoers hiking beside the vehicles became a flood, spilling into stuffed parking lots, which appeared to have been carved from the jutting earth.

Early in our courtship, Richard and I had learned we would be unable to see Paul Simon play at the venue nearest us, Maryland's Merriweather Post Pavilion. Though we were both disappointed, I felt particularly down, having never seen Simon—who was then seventy-five—in concert. In a spontaneous act consistent with his typical generosity, Richard suggested that we should instead travel to Denver at the end of the month for Simon's last stop on the tour: Red Rocks Ampitheatre. The idea of flying most of the way across the country to see a concert—even Paul Simon at Red Rocks—

seemed egregiously extravagant. Still, when the first strains of accordion floated up from the stage below and the crowd fell quiet, I knew why I had come.

Simon began with "The Boy in the Bubble," the track that opens *Graceland* and is also indelibly inscribed upon me. By the time that first drumbeat punctuated the accordion's initial jive, I was leaning into Richard, feeling the synthesis of a lifetime of music roll through my body. Once the bass guitar began to lead with its honking-tuba boogie, I was reliving my whole life inside Simon's song.

Sunset, when it came, danced burnt-orange and golden across the Colorado landscape, beyond the natural amphitheatre in which we stood. As the sun's angle lowered, the gigantic rocks surrounding our stadium seats changed colors—red, rust, sepia—and cast unexpected shadows. We swayed, inhaling the rhythm of Simon's music—all 9,525 of us. The show sold out; not a surprise for the final stop on Paul Simon's second-to-last tour. The audience alliance was palpable, and Simon could feel it, too.

His seventeen-song set list included four from *Graceland*, and Simon rolled out the title track during his first encore— when heartily pressed, he returned for *three* encores, leaving his unbelieving audience stunned with gratitude. That night, Simon played my three favorites from his well-loved album—"The Boy in the Bubble," "That Was Your Mother," and "Graceland" itself—as well as "Diamonds on the Soles of Her Shoes" and "You Can Call Me Al," all of which hit the cool high-desert air with practiced precision. Hundreds of miles from both my western Maine hometown and my West Virginia farm, holding tight to the hand of a man I barely knew, I was home.

■ ■ ■

I must have been very young the first time I heard the *Graceland* album; Simon's music was woven into my childhood in a way that has left me ignorant of the practical facts. My mother, Sarah, recalls that my father first spun the *Graceland* cassette on repeat in the dash of his green-and-tan Ford F-150 Custom. Choad remembers that it was my mother who was enamored of Simon's release, and that the beige- and primary-hued record album first resided on our open music shelf at home. Either way, by the time I could walk and talk—and, believe me, I was precocious—every lick and lyric of *Graceland* was on file in my little mulleted head.

With the simple verse "My traveling companion is nine years old / He is the child of my first marriage," Simon offers his listener pieces of his own fractured history, and the complications of his present, which, it seems, propel him over that road, son by his side, "going to Graceland." The vulnerability he offers allows the listener to connect: interior to interior, hurt touching hurt, loss identifying with fear.

Soon enough, I was that child of nine, not Simon's, but—perhaps like his son Harper—tumbling in the wake of divorce, gasping for my breath. My brother Owen and I were stricken by the awareness that we, too, were the product of a first marriage—and devastated to discover that marriages could end, that families could shift form from comfortable to the chaos of lugging schoolwork, clothes, and favorite things from one home to the next. We had little consistency to cling to, but we did have music, and each other.

Yet, Simon's auditory alchemy continued to work on my own little wounded heart during those tender years. I became sure that, somehow, I was a part of that song, *Graceland*'s title track, even though the "he" did not fit, because the age and heartache did. Paul Simon did more than help me learn that I could connect to music: he shared the secrets of what had been and the prognosis of what was to be. As Simon admitted to *Rolling Stone*'s David Fricke: "Hope and dread . . . that's the way I see the world—a balance between the two, but coming down on the side of hope."

Simon wrote *Graceland* shortly after his brief second marriage to the actress Carrie Fisher dissolved in 1984. They continued to see each other on occasion, though, through the end of the decade and, as Fisher later told *Rolling Stone*, "'Graceland' has part of us in it." That "us" sits squarely in the second verse: "She comes back to tell me she's gone" hits me plumb in the heart every time I hear it. Simon's words illuminate my own father's pain, embody the confusion inherent in loss, echo details that a former lover may never forget. Simon sings of being haunted by the strange emptiness of his bed, the micro-memory of how his sweetheart swept her hair back from her forehead. Which minutiae replayed in my father's mind? I see him, set abruptly adrift, rushing from room to room in that vast house he built by hand, snapping photos of the intricate hemlock woodwork he would never see again.

Yesterday, as I spoke with my mother through the long line of our telephones, I mentioned that the only recollection I have of her and my father together is of the day they told my brother and me that they would be divorcing. The edges of this memory are fuzzy, perhaps dissolved from too much close peering, an excess of reflective scrutiny over the years, but I do remember that it was necessary for them to not only reveal their decision to separate, but to explain divorce as a concept to their seven- and five-year-old children.

My brother is sure that our parents called us downstairs to talk, that we sat on the two couches that framed the sunroom, that Mom spoke while my father stood, removed, perhaps in the kitchen. Or maybe my mother's memory—of fashioning a fat nest of pillows in the bedroom that my parents no longer would share—is accurate: "I tried to make it nice, so you could feel cozy; gathering you like a mama with her chicks," she says. "Your dad was not there, I don't think."

Choad, though, was most definitely present, because he—more than any of us—recalls the tragic sadness: "It was fucking horrible; you guys just about died. It was the worst day of my life, pretty much, when that happened—it was sad and un-fucking-believable. Little Brillo-headed Owen, and you." I can hear him hanging his head, wavering from side to side, as he presses the telephone to his ear. My heartbroken father cannot even recount what happened that day, now over thirty years ago, because the anguish feels too tender, too fresh. The pain of divorce still haunts him, but the trauma of seeing his children floating out into an unknown ocean remains more than Choad can bear.

What I am sure about is this: my mother did the talking, because she was the one who wanted the divorce. My father, big-hearted and loyal to the end, agreed to present the decision as mutual, but his body rebelled—forcing him to stand, or pace, or make himself so faint that he disappeared from my mother's memory of that day entirely. I have no doubt that Owen sat silent, kindergarten mind a-whirling, hidden behind his short-cropped hair and big chocolate eyes.

"I remember you two, sitting there with your little minds and your little hearts, trying to understand it. I remember feeling like I had just broken open the egg and it was running all over the floor and there was no putting it back together," recalls my mother. "It always seemed changeable when I was talking with your dad about it, but once we told you, it felt done. It all felt very grave and serious and final and permanent."

What strikes me most is the similarity; the way my mother, who initiated the separation, experienced such an intense feeling of powerlessness. Her words to me today—"I felt like I was tumbling down a tube and I couldn't stop and go back up"—could have been spoken by my father on that day, as he stood, paralyzed by grief, just outside of the sunroom. My brother, too, sitting stone-silent and as still as our father, felt his young heart flip-flop as it fell off the cliff. And I can see my girlhood self—mute, for once—mouth agape, gasping for the precious air my stunned lungs could not draw.

Still, I am sure that my parents—both of them, because Choad would have rallied for this—joined voices to, again, speak into being the chorus of our childhood: "We will *always* love you, we will *always* love you, we will *always* love you." And, now that we had entered a reality where extra reassurance was needed, a new refrain: "This is *not* your fault, this is *not* your fault, this is *not* your fault."

And I can see my girlhood self—mute, for once— mouth agape, gasping for the precious air my stunned lungs could not draw.

I do not remember what Owen did, but I ran up to my room and cried in my closet, snapping off slabs of sheetrock from the unfinished door jamb and eating them—seeking solace any way I could find it.

When, later, that unified front of mutual decision revealed itself as an ill-fitting cover for my mother's unilateral choice to separate, this seemed like a less convenient but more honest telling. Decades after, when I found myself divorcing— thankfully, without children—I could again see a greater part of the whole story. My own divorce granted me clarity about the nuances of connection and promise—and experience with the public pain that Simon cites: how a window in the heart flies open when love breaks. How "Everybody sees you're blown apart / Everybody sees the wind blow." As a child, I witnessed these wages of loss as our comfortable familial love—the undoubtable thread of my childhood—turned cold, turned off like a faucet.

I doubt my mother ever echoed Simon's words (which could have been Fisher's) to my father, but I do know for sure that everybody saw him get blown apart; everybody saw the wind blow through that wide-open heart of his.

■ ■ ■

Choad, despite surviving what amounted to a forced divorce, chose to keep his heart open. Sure, he sought a resurrection of romantic love—and found it, again and again— but he also loved his kids with such fierce dedication that he never missed an opportunity to show up for us. He wrought weekends and every other Wednesday night into festivity. Although I am sure it was not easy to balance self-employment, a girlfriend, spirituality, and fatherhood, he did it—and humor was essential to the way he parented. It still is.

We would be riding in his truck, that same F-150 Custom with the greasy bench seat and brown bananas on the dash, and the striking Zydeco of "That Was Your Mother" would swing into rotation, as the B-side of the Graceland cassette eased toward its end:

> *A long time ago, yeah*
> *Before you was born, dude*
> *When I was still single*
> *And life was great*

Choad, raising and wiggling his eyebrows while reaching over to tickle the knees of whichever unlucky kid was stuck in the middle seat—even as he continued to drive with his left hand through the steering wheel and keep perfect tempo on the dashboard drums—would embody Simon, ribbing us both for simultaneously ruining and imbuing meaning into his life. We knew we were "the burden of [his] generation," but our father also made sure we knew he loved us.

At the time, wedged in the tangle of knees, gearshift, banana and body odor, and arguments about airflow—*windows down! windows up!*—I had no idea how powerfully this memory would cling to my psyche.

If we were in that truck, we were listening to music. Choad sang along to it all—intoning with the *a cappella*, beating the dash with the rhythm of the drums, miming Simon and his many clever vocalizations. With such a dedicated teacher offering his example, no wonder my brother and I internalized our father's full-throated, whole-body habit of how best to interact with tunes. Now, when I recall my goofy father alternating between serenading and teasing my brother and me, I feel the wash of family, the same imperfect filial love that Simon and his young son bore over the road.

Memory, though, is a slippery substance, especially in early life. Once my parents separated, the changing shape of our family began to play tricks on my child-mind. Home became a feeling, rather than one static place. Before the divorce was final, my mother had both outwitted a diagnosis of pancreatic cancer and found her spiritual calling as a Jehovah's Witness. We learned to live with a different set of rules in each household. Within a few short years, Owen and I had gained an abusive stepfather and lost all connection with our mother. Our father's love remained constant, but trauma had forever changed our family. While my young heart and mind were preoccupied with holding on, *Graceland* slipped into my subconscious.

■ ■ ■

I am eleven and outside on a familiar, sloping lawn near
Barnstable, Massachusetts, on Cape Cod. The hour is late
enough that the ocean mist arcs along the curve of the yard,
but not so late that my bare feet are freezing. I am surrounded
by children and adults I love—people I trust implicitly, most
of whom I have known all my life. My father, my brother, and I
see this group of people every August, often in this very place,
always for this very occasion: we call it Bow-Wow Boogie.
For decades, a motley group—academics, artists, carpenters,
writers, farmers, and musicians—who first bonded in late
1960s Cambridge has been making the trek for a weekend of
rowdy play each year.

The rules of Bow-Wow are simple: drink on Friday night,
play softball on Saturday—the best of three games wins and
the losing team buys the beer for Saturday night—drink again,
and then roll out of the tent and into the car to head home on
Sunday. While I did turn out to be an alcoholic, I did very little
actual drinking at Bow-Wow, because my conscience was too
potent to steal and I was too young for anyone decent to want
to share their stash. No matter—the games, food, once-a-year
visiting, music, and storytelling were intoxicating enough.

This evening, I am on the lawn, having just wolfed down
too much meaty spaghetti, holding a sweaty death-grip on
hands to either side, chanting, "Red Rover, Red Rover, let...
Otis come over!" and bracing for the impact as Otis, running
at full speed, attempts to break through our clasped hands,
hoping we can hold him so that he must, by the rules of
the game, join our team. Music wafts through the salty air,
piped out of the house through a complex maze of wires
and speakers. The stereo plays, but my ears are not engaged;
music is part of the ambient noise of the place. In an instant,

all of that changes—with the first bars of some unmistakable song, something that speaks to my soul in a way that I cannot explain, but also cannot identify—accordion and drums and then punchy brass, and then the vocals begin: "It was a slow day and the sun was beating on the soldiers by the side of the road..."

Impossibly, I know every word; I am singing along in my head, lost from the game of Red Rover. I break away, then, eliciting protests and confusion from our poor, dwindling team. "I'll be right back," I say, unsure if I am telling the truth.

I wander across the yard—dusk has fallen and I squint, peering through the night, trying to find my father among the many mingling, laughing adults. In my head, my brain, which has somehow detached itself from my control, continues to tick through the lyrics and timing of the song, which is winding down as I recognize the shape and posture of my father. "Choad—" I begin, and he, perhaps hearing the worry in my voice, turns aside from the group with which he is talking, "—what is this music?" I see a faintly confused look on his face, as he tips his head slightly to one side.

"It's *Graceland*. Paul Simon." And then, kindly, questioning, "You know that."

But I didn't know—even though my brain knew every lyric, all of the breaks, ebbs, and rises. Perhaps *Graceland* had fallen out of rotation for a time, maybe the cassette was sliding around under the seat of the truck, gathering crud, instead of tucked into its felted slot inside Choad's brown leather cassette briefcase. This was during the post-divorce period, before circumstances indicated that I needed to live with my father full-time, and that, by default, my brother would come along. Simon must not have made the playlist for Wednesday nights and weekends that year, or the year before. Whatever had caused the rift, *Graceland* and I were officially reunited.

That Sunday, we listened to the cassette all the way home from Cape Cod.

■ ■ ■

So many songwriters write lyrics for other musicians to sing; many singers give voice to others' words. Simon's role as both writer and singer allows him to project the lyrics in the exact way in which he first heard them play in his own head and heart. This is especially evident in places where Simon's own wordplay slips off of his tongue in such precise, lyrical rhythm, as it does in the third verse of "Graceland" when Simon sings about "falling, flying, tumbling in turmoil," connecting his own personal anarchy with the abstract lyrical image of girl-as-human-trampoline. An unforgettable New York City girl, who—as Simon told *SongTalk Magazine*—is entirely made-up, the line having popped into his head as he walked past the Museum of Natural History. "It's not related to anybody. Or anything. It just struck me as funny. Although that's an image that people remember, they talk about that line."

For me—a girl living far from New York City—the idea of embodying a trampoline was irresistible. My first friend, Caitlin—another Bow-Wow Boogie kid—was in proud possession of one of the ubiquitous large-diameter trampolines of the nineties. We spent incalculable hours bouncing, lazing, and perfecting our imperfect gymnastics and pre-teen attitudes on its slick black surface, sometimes peering, bellies down, through the powerful, taut steel springs or over the rounded blue edging at the moss and rock three feet below.

We talked, we played, we teased Owen without mercy for his only—and entirely earnest—shortcoming: "You are SO un-soph!" Seeing his confusion at our clever abbreviation, we would collapse into giggling fits, unaware that his degree of sophistication was, in reality, very much akin to ours, given that all three of us were growing up as communal siblings-of-sorts at the long end of a skinny road in the rural Maine woods. Owen was nothing if not forgiving, though, and magnanimous to the core, so bare minutes would pass before the three of us, reunified, would slide off the trampoline and patter, barefooted, along the dark earth path to the cool of Spear Stream for a shallow swim before dinner.

The soundtrack to our play crackled out through yards of threaded line from the leviathan sound system housed between stacks of record albums and folds of batik wall hangings in Caitlin's farmhouse living room. Deep blues, mostly—Muddy Waters, Johnny Winter, Memphis Slim—but also The Rolling Stones, The Allman Brothers, and Canned Heat. Paul Simon's *Graceland* was a favorite of Caitlin's mother, Devon, but curating tunes was one of the few household tasks in which she did not have a regular hand, so Simon rarely made it into rotation.

That trampoline, though, was central to my youth, and a cornerstone of connection with the imaginary girl in Simon's New York City, and thus *Graceland* as a whole. In just a few short years, that ten-year-old on the trampoline would have her first taste of "falling, flying, tumbling in turmoil," but it would be many years yet before I would reach the end of the stanza, to find myself "bouncing into Graceland."

■ ■ ■

As the song "Graceland" winds down, repetition, another dear friend of the songwriter, makes Simon shine in the act of his craft. In verse, where repetition is not necessarily expected, Simon offers a refrain of his lover's statement, now internalized, made his own: "And I see losing love is like a window in your heart."

When—clean and sober at twenty-three, for the first time in ten wild years—I searched my surroundings for my self, trying to jigsaw the pieces back into place, Simon's insight returned. As lost wisdom is wont to do—alcoholics call it a moment of clarity—*Graceland* surfaced in my consciousness, like the soothing ease of ice on a bad burn. Simon's lyrical assurance that we all will be welcome in *Graceland* spoke straight to my battered heart in the same way that recovery had begun to do.

Whether despite or because of its many pat sayings and iterative clichés—*you are not alone, we will love you until you can love yourself, you are right where you are supposed to be*—recovery seemed like an attractive option when compared with the mess of the decade before. What I had mistaken as

Graceland surfaced in my consciousness, like the soothing ease of ice on a bad burn. Simon's lyrical assurance that we all will be welcome in Graceland spoke straight to my battered heart...

a love of getting high had revealed itself to be, instead, about power and control. With each dawn, a new beginning; with every meeting I attended, I felt a little more sure of who I was, and—surprisingly—the curious girl I had buried under years of using and the lies that supported my habit began to resurrect herself. For me, those days were the embodiment of Simon's "miracle and wonder." I had, in the past year, transitioned from addicted to recovering—*hopeless dope fiend to dopeless hope fiend.* Life felt new and different every day: like there was something to discover, as if anything could happen, and the unexpected did happen, repeatedly.

■ ■ ■

Late August in Arizona, no matter the day, is hot. Prescott, with its perfect Wild West downtown—a granite courthouse situated mid-square—and high-desert atmosphere, is not exempt from the heat. I am buzzing with anticipation as I walk the few blocks from my home, which is in complete disarray as I pack for the cross-country drive that will make it, officially, no longer my home. Hold Fast Tattoo is a few doors down from the bright back alley where I help a local farm set up their CSA tables on weekday afternoons, where I pick up my raw milk share: glass gallons, straight from the cooler, sweating in the sun. This is to be my first tattoo; though I had planned it years before, any extra money always went to feed my drug habit, or to repair the damage after yet another night of drunk driving. My friend Angeline knows the place, and the guy: he inked a plump, orange Ganesha on her upper arm the year before, and now she swears by his talent.

I am looking for something a little quieter, without color but with connection—not to another culture but to the roots of my own raising. My anticipation is so high that I arrive on time, for once, but tattoo shop time, apparently, is like island time. I find an uncomfortable chair wedged in the way of everyone in the shop and wait it out, hoping my aloof appearance will help me fit in, despite my still-virgin skin.

While I sit, I recirculate the good reasons I have for getting this tattoo and try not to think about how upset my mother, with whom I have reconciled, will be. *I am making this decision with a clear, sober head. This is a tattoo that I have been planning for years. It connects me to both of my parents. It connects me to my home, and the music of my life. The truth—I really want to be cool, and it seems so much easier to achieve that in ink*—is harder to access. Before I have the chance to spin myself into a high-tilt tizzy, I hear: "You ready?"

I nod, perhaps dishonestly: "Yes."

Novice that I am, I do not expect the process to take so long. Today is a repeat of the preparative steps we took the week before, when I came into the shop, ready for action, and left with a mock-up in blue ink along my spine. "Think about it," he said, "because the spine is one of the most painful places to get a tattoo. I don't want to get halfway through and have you bail on me."

This time, though, it will be for real. And once he starts, for real, it does hurt—just as much as he promised—but I focus on my breathing and do my best to act nonchalant when he checks to make sure I am not going to pass out. I remember how I tricked my mother and father, separately, into penning the words that this tall, quiet man is now inking, indelibly, onto my spine. How my Armageddon-focused mother's part—*These are the days*—fit neatly and also so impossibly with my wide-eyed, New Age father's portion—*of miracle and wonder*. I consider how perturbed each of them will be when they find out—not just about the tattoo, but also the deception inherent in inking the words in their handwriting—my father, briefly and easily; my mother, pensively and perhaps forever.

After what may be the longest three hours of my life, the artist stands up, stretches his shoulders, and nods his approval. As I rise, slowly finding the lost strength in my legs, he indicates the mirrors that frame his station, suggesting that I take a look. I see jeans, a long, bare torso, and my black lace brassiere before twisting hips and shoulders to reveal smudges of blue ink, a hint of blood, and the first line of the chorus of "Boy in the Bubble" imbedded forever on my body. I nod to my reflection, as if acknowledging embodiment of Simon's truth.

I feel like a new person, as if I have crossed some invisible threshold, like smoking pot for the first time. A coming of age, of sorts: I have joined my marked-up generation at last. I pay for the tattoo, adding a proper tip as my mother taught me, and pull down my black T-shirt before stepping out into the fading high-desert sun. As I drift home, I feel Simon's poetry sinking into my skin, the early evening abuzz with the miracle and wonder we share. ■

LEARNING TO DRIVE A STICK

Dad never taught me how to drive a stick,
and too many times I had stripped the gears
off my brothers' trucks when they had an afternoon of patience.
My Grandad, too, used to flood the clutch—
and by that I mean, he drove his Ford Pinto into the neighbor's pond.
The sheriff decided to stop letting him drive drunk after that.
In the hospital, the detective asked in curt English
why I didn't leave after someone
slammed me into a concrete ledge
using the fist of a rented Skoda.

I thought,
I don't know why I'm with my boyfriend either—
the muscle of my *no* had atrophied,
as it had in Granny's legs back in Kentucky.
Drinking and smashed fenders
have the same nose for my family as high cholesterol.
In the night after,
I did what the lady with the stale perfume at those Al Anon meetings said,
let him tread through his own decisions
but who would choose to stand on the shore and
watch arms cut through dark empty waters?

He tried to climb the fire escape drunk after I locked up the soft,
empty dark of my apartment to keep him from
re-emerging, dripping wet in my bed.
He slipped.
That's how I knew he was there,
his nails made a *tschk* sound as he dug into the metal ladder,
boots grazing back over the grating of the footholds.
I carried him down from the landing where he puddled.

Do not ask me how I carried a man down a fire escape.
Granny said I was always too skinny—weak
she meant, never ate enough, but she oversalted
everything: biscuits, beans, coffee—
Dad told me she poured in the salt to cut Grandad's hangovers.
She thought she could dry up the slug in him.

He used to hit her—not *him*, not *me*.
Grandad used to hit Granny.
Not just with his fists: that's why,
even after he's been dead for longer than
I've been alive, we eat supper off plastic plates.

After I drug him into the safety of the elevator,
I hit him. Not him, *him*.
In the morning he doesn't remember, but God I wish he did—
I wish he knew what the meat of my fists tasted like,
what it felt like to be mashed into the size of my palm,
so he could know what it's like to be a passenger.

I slept in the bathroom so I could lock the door.
I heard him in my little bed.
I could hear him piss in my little bed.
I heard him roll over, fall off my little bed, groan, gurgle—
then heard nothing at all.

I wish I could hit him. Not *him*—Grandad.
I wish I was alive when they dredged up his Ford Pinto,
the stocked catfish still flopping in the chapped leather of the backseats.

If I was the one to have found him, I'd have drug him
to the grass bank and whaled on him
till I'd killed that part that would've born me
so I'd never have to learn to drive a stick,

never have to fail at driving a stick,
never have to be stuck, flooding the engine, mashing
the clutch, shifting from first to third and lurching back instead.
If I never had to learn how to drive a stick, I'd never have to
hate someone so much that I would lay on the cool gloss of the tile
and think about what would happen if I stayed in the bathroom, closed
my eyes while he—who I promised my forever,
would drown in a teacup's worth of sick.

Two of the paramedics that carried him out nodded down to him,
He looks like the Marlboro Man.
Was that why I stayed?
Another paramedic hung back to speak in the stairwell,
It's not your fault.
Would Granny have wanted to kiss her like I had?
Or would she have stared back blankly, finished scraping
congealed beans from plastic plates as if she'd
never considered such a thing in her life...

MAKAYLA GAY

CARPENTER CEMETERY

We approached death with full plates.
Once the cicadas fell
from their slick resin
we drove Chevrolets full
up to the hill.

Us kids squatted out of sight
to pluck legs off daddy long's
till the preaching and tinny singing
stopped, and we answered by
tearing free, screaming — wild
like banshees, like the ones our
family left-back on a further hill.

I've never used to think of death and dying.
I only thought of biscuits still warm
in their tin and smiling in pretty
dresses next to cousins who didn't
have to climb up the hill this year.

MAKAYLA GAY

NEEMA AVASHIA

In truth, I've always felt uneasy in my relationship to the word 'Appalachian'... do you not count if you are Brown, Indian, the child of immigrants who moved to a place out of necessity again thirty years later, when work disappeared?" Neema Avashia writes in *Another Appalchia: Coming Up Queer and Indian in a Mountain Place,* her debut essay collection.

Published in March by West Virginia University Press, the book explores the economic decline in her West Virginia hometown, the struggles to represent her intersecting identities, and the significant relationships that shaped her as a child in Appalachia. Avashia's work has been published *The Bitter Southerner, The Kenyon Review Online, Still: The Journal,* and other magazines. Avashia spoke with writer and *Appalachian Review* student assistant Skylar Bensheimer to discuss her new essay collection.

■ ■ ■

SKYLAR BENSHEIMER: I wanted to start with the opening essay, "Directions to a Vanishing Place." It feels like a natural way to start the collection, especially with the second person and the directives. Did you know you wanted to begin the collection with that essay?

NEEMA AVASHIA: Yes, largely because it was the first essay I wrote in the collection. It was the first essay to be published, the first essay that set the direction for what I was going to do. For readers who are unfamiliar, I felt like I needed to ground them in the place, and I felt like there wasn't another way to do that besides taking them there. If I start with this idea of directions and I locate you in the place, then with everything that comes after, there's less burden to establish place. It still has to happen to some extent, but it's less of a need in other essays if I do a good job in that first essay.

SB: In the opening pages, you listed when and where each essay had been published before, and they were all published in the last couple of years. It's also a relatively short book, but you still cover a lot of subjects and touch

Neema Avashia

on a lot of topics. What was the process like when you were compiling these essays? Were there cuts that you had to make?

NA: It was actually the opposite. It wasn't so much cutting as it was figuring out if there was enough there for a collection. I have a mentor, Geeta Kothari, who's a professor at the University of Pittsburgh, and she said, "You need 50,000 words. You can't do anything with this until you have at least 50,000 words." So, there were some ways where I thought, *Okay. I'm going to see if I have enough things to say that can get me to 50,000 words and that can feel like a complete collection.* It wasn't so much cutting as it was writing to a goal or writing to a place where I felt like I had a complete collection.

SB: One of the through-lines that really interested me in the book was this theme of isolation, whether that is being a minority in a conservative, mostly white area, the move from rural West Virginia to Boston, where you describe neighbors not really knowing each other, or when you write about the pandemic. Would you characterize those experiences as isolating, or do you think of them in a different way?

NA: I think "isolating" is the right word for them. It's taken me a long time to understand, but when you're somebody whose identity is so intersectional, it can be really hard to find places where you don't feel isolated because even if one or two parts of you are represented, the thing that starts to surface for you is the thing that's not represented. That becomes the thing I'm most aware of. There are not a lot of places where queerness, Appalachian-ness, and Indian-ness are held together, and because of that you can end up in disconnects where people can see parts of you, and they can understand parts of you, but they don't necessarily understand all of you. I talk about that a lot in the book. My family very much understands the Appalachian and Indian parts of me, but the queer part is a thing that they're still trying to figure out. You can even trick yourself into feeling like you're really close, but then something will happen that will remind you that you're not as close as you thought you were because there's a disconnect again. Isolation is a thing that I feel like I've experienced a lot in both trying to establish

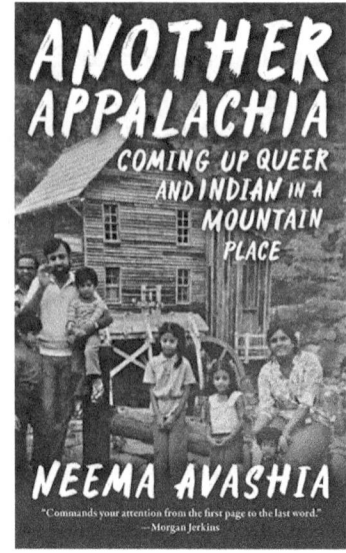

strong connections with people but also seeing where those connections fray or can become tenuous because the visibility of all parts of my identity isn't held in a space.

SB: You mentioned establishing relationships, and it seems like that's how you characterize your connections to Appalachian places and cultures—through the relationships that you have with people rather than through land and geography. Is that how you'd also define your place in Boston, or is there a different emphasis on geography there?

NA: Living in Boston, I actually feel more connected to Appalachian geography. The day before yesterday I was in West Virginia, and I am so aware that I live on the coast now, and so aware of how I think coastal geography makes people different. When you're in the mountains, you know you're really small. You're reminded of how small you are all the time, and when you live on the coast, you don't always have that humility because you don't have the mountains around you saying, "You're not as big as you think you are." In a way, my appreciation and awareness of how Appalachian geography shaped me was heightened once I left and once I became aware of what it's like to live in a place where there are no mountains. How much less grounded do I feel because I don't have those mountains around me? The through-line in every place where I've lived that I think is a significant result of growing up in Appalachia is the relationships. I learned how to build relationships from people in Appalachia, and that is something that I have carried throughout my whole life, that way of knowing people and seeing people, connecting with people, supporting people. Everything I know about how to be a good human and take care of other people, I learned at home, I learned growing up. That is the driver even in my Boston life. People think I'm very strange because that's not how other people in Boston behave, but the way I build relationships is probably the most Appalachian part of me.

SB: Returning to the theme of isolation, you also talk about social media in the essays. Especially in the last couple of years, it can both serve as a connection between people, but it's also a way for people to blindly spew hatred without having to reckon with those actions. With Mr. B you describe this as a "lost ability" to see each other. Has your relationship with social media changed at all? Is there a healthy way to navigate it currently?

NA: There could be. I think part of what happened during the most intense period of this pandemic, when things were locked down, is that people were being reduced to their social media presence, which was already happening before but got even worse. Before that, someone could be spewing ridiculousness on social media, but you would see them. And those moments when you saw each other in person, and you had three-dimensional bodies and feelings and experiences, could mitigate whatever intensity was happening online.

Then we went into this time when we were actually physically isolated and socially isolated from each other and didn't have those in-person interactions to do the mitigating anymore. Everybody gets flattened. Everybody gets reduced. There are so many things said online—and I would put entire paychecks on this—that no one would say out loud. Most people I know believe themselves to be decent people and would not utter the phrases out loud to someone that they will post online about that person's identity. But you weren't seeing those people, and you weren't getting that check telling you that this isn't a decent way to behave. That exacerbated what had already started. It's not new. 2015 and 2016 was when we saw this intensify. It could be healthy if we could hold it in the balance of physically connecting with people and then having social media connections with those people, but when it's all online, I don't know that it can be good.

That said, I'm on book tour right now, and one of the neat things about it is I'm meeting people who I only knew online prior to this, people who I connected with on Twitter because they're Appalachian folks, because Appalachian Twitter is the best Twitter. They're people I connected with because we shared interests and we shared ideas, and now I got to see them in person. That was really lovely. Being able to put a three-dimensional being behind a face or handle or ideas has been powerful for me. If we were not thinking about social media as a substitute for meaningful interaction but as a support for meaningful interaction, meaningful in-person interaction, it could be ok, but we ended up in a situation where social media is the only interaction, and I don't think that's a good space.

SB: I completely agree. I'm a big basketball fan and enjoyed reading your essay, "Be Like Wilt." You later write about reading that essay at the Hindman Settlement School and being unsure if that would resonate with people. That reading turns out well, but has that been a rare connection for you elsewhere—the literary world and the basketball world? They can seem disparate at times.

NA: It's not weird in Appalachia. One of the coolest things about reading that essay at Hindman was how many people didn't "know" Carl Bradford but *knew* Carl Bradford. They had *a* Carl Bradford. Especially in rural places, sports are a formative part of a lot of peoples' identities, and it isn't until you get older that you feel like these are polar lines where you're either a sports person or you're an arts person. Growing up I didn't feel like that was a binary or that I had to choose. When I've shared that essay with people who aren't sports people, the thing they're able to resonate with is the idea of mentorship and the idea that people who aren't your blood family can play such a formative role in developing who you are as a person. That's been a hook for people who, if they aren't basketball people, can find a way into it. I actually pick that essay a lot for readings because I think it's a good one to bring people into the space. Even if you're not a sports person, the image of this scrawny kid who can't make a basket is an underdog story you can root for. I rely on those elements of it—the relationship, the underdog story—to hold onto people for whom basketball isn't as interesting of a concept.

SB: You write about an "Indo-lachian" identity, but you also describe a potential exodus of Indian families from West Virginia after your parents' generation. If Indo-lachians are, as you describe, a "demographic anomaly" in West Virginia, how do you hope that your story and your history resonate with other communities?

NA: This points to the title of the book, but so often in mainstream narratives about Appalachia that don't come from [the region], Appalachia is reduced to white, Christian, straight, and homogenous. When I wrote this [book], it wasn't necessarily that I thought that I was only going to represent this Indian-American experience. Part of what I was hoping to do was to point out that Appalachia is a much more complicated place. There are immigrant communities that have been there for a long time. There's a Black community that has been there since before West Virginia was a state. There's a diversity and a complexity to Appalachia that it isn't afforded a lot of the time. The book that became a bestseller and was on the bestseller list for fifty-one weeks doesn't complicate that narrative about Appalachia at all. There are tons of other writers who do. There are queer Appalachian writers, Black Appalachian writers, and Indigenous Appalachian writers who are putting out amazing books but they're not the ones who are getting plastered on the front page of the *New York Times*.

I think a lot of people outside of Appalachia are invested in perpetuating these stereotypes and this flattened understanding of Appalachia. My hope by writing this book was to make people pause on that stereotyping. Right from the outset, when they look at the cover, I want their understandings to be upended. In the image you can see: It's clearly a rural place. It's clearly in the fall. It's clearly in Appalachia, but the people standing in front of Babcock mill are the members of my extended Indian family. I want this book to plant enough seeds to make you think, *well, if there are Indian people there, there are probably other people there, too. I can't just have this flat view of this place anymore.* ■

GATHERING HICKORY NUTS
BEFORE THE EXAMINATION

This time of year, the morning fog—cloaking rain
or sun—makes no promises. But come what may,
there's always work to be done: dead-head the marigolds,
survey the garden, removing what no longer fruits.

Instead, you rattle the mower into position and pull
the cord for the last cut of the season. Soon, the dull
blades are knocking off the dark brown husks of hickory
nuts that have dropped, then rolled, from the tree—

some, all the way to the road. The rest—spit out
as hard white shells you'll gather to crack, but not
before dumping in water to tell the good from the bad,
keeping the ones that sink. After lunch, sit on the crinkly

white paper of the examination table until the doctor
comes in, asks you to lie back, then begins to press
his fingertips beneath your ribcage (*yes*, you say, *but
it's always tender where they took it away*) to just above

your pelvis (*and* there, *where it came back*). Don't ask,
How long? You get what you get. Knock the hulls off
a hundred lives and most will float like ghosts; they're
shriveled and hollow before they even hit the ground.

BILL KING

POST-DIAGNOSIS

When I moved to this town, there was a man who shuffled up
and down the drag—slow as a tugboat pulling an invisible load.
His head slumped but he kept his blue twill work shirt ironed

and matching pants cinched tight. Once, when I passed him
on the street and nodded, he stopped, looked me in the eyes,
and made the sound of a kid-size motor bike that goes round

and round. Now, I understand that no one really understands.
It's why, at the end of the block, rather than leaning into the turn
as I have for years, I keep going, into a field hemmed and

humming with rose. Once cleared for cows that sunk fetlock deep
in this creek, now it's blackberry and wingstem. Here and there
a pokeweed—blood red and heavy with fruit. You have to find

a deer trail through—a chest-high crease that catches at clothing,
then closes behind as you go. Today is hot and humid. Cicada,
like a pressure canner thrumming on the stove, and over that,

the cry of two sharp-shins, then crows. Like them, I want to tell
you what I feel. I want words to see me through. In the cool
of the wood, a young doe watches. She's waiting for me to move.

BILL KING

ORANGE SODA

LEO COFFEY

Dan is fifteen and almost a foot taller than me. Even though I'm only six years younger, he thinks it's funny to call me a kid. Our daddies cut grass together, so in the summer we spend a lot of time with each other. We like to shoot BB guns at the neighbor's cats and swim in the creek behind my house. Sometimes we sneak into my daddy's closet and hold the real heavy guns while we look in the mirror, but I always get nervous doing that. I think because my grandpa once told me about how he watched a man get his head blown clean off in Vietnam. I never could get the image of that man's neck spewing blood like a fountain out of my head. Sometimes when it storms, I dream about that man walking up behind me. I never fail to wake up just before I turn around, but I always know that it is him.

It is one of those hot summer days in Ellenboro, North Carolina, like strip your clothes off as soon as you walk out the door hot. There seems to be no end in sight to our friendship as Dan and I make our way down US-74 on foot. We don't talk much; we just walk with our T-shirts pulled up over our heads to let some air onto our skin. My belly button pokes out like a budded flower.

When we make it to the KwikStop, the parking lot is empty minus an old white Honda Accord parked by the air pump. I can hear The Lake playing a tribute to Whitney Houston from the speakers, the soft tune of her asking, "Where do broken hearts go? Can they find their way home?" She died earlier this week, and everybody's momma was torn up about it.

I sit outside on the bench to the left of the door while Dan goes inside. Dan wants to get a soda before we walk to his house a half-mile further. He doesn't tell me that he doesn't have any money. There are piles of ash sitting along the bench and I lean down and blow them off one at a time, watching the wind redeposit every particle onto the asphalt.

After a few minutes, the door creaks open and Dan walks out. He sits down next to me and lifts his shirt to reveal a bulged can shoved deep into his pants pocket. He cracks open the aluminum and takes a long sip like he hasn't ever had anything to drink in his life. His nose scrunches up as the liquid tunnels down his throat. He swallows hard and takes a deep breath to make room in his mouth for words.

"Damn! That's good shit," he says. He places the can on the pavement by his feet and removes a Snickers from his pocket. Sweat falls like shadows on the floor from the black hair that curtains his forehead. He devours the candy bar in a few bites and tosses the wrapper over his shoulder. It falls to the ground like a leaf.

"You ever stolen anything, Clint?" Dan asks.

I say no.

"Why not? Think you're too good for it?"

I say no.

He takes a blade out of his pocket with his free hand and unfolds my fingers to place its metal weight into mine. My eyes grow wide with surprise.

"I want you to go in there and steal something. Anything you want. And if that lady behind the counter says anything, you flash her this knife," he says.

I say I can't do that. I tell him it's wrong.

"What's more wrong–going hungry and dying of thirst? Or stealing?"

I say nothing.

"Fine. Well, you ain't having none of my orange soda, and you can turn around and go on home, too."

It is hot as piss outside. I can feel myself growing more fatigued the longer we sit in the heat. I don't want to walk back by myself. I'd only ever done that once, and I ended up crying on some lady's porch until she finally came home an hour later and drove me back to my house. Nobody was home when we got there, so I just laid in the front yard and watched the clouds roll by.

The bells above the door ring and a guy walks out and hops in his car. I stand up and shove the blade into my pocket. Dan smiles and takes another swig of soda. I want so badly to prove myself to him and show him I'm a man. I figure I don't have anything to lose.

"Be ready to run if things go south," he says.

I nod on my way towards the door and swing it open. The bell rattles above me and the lady behind the counter smiles and waves. She has dark skin and is big-chested with beetle-black beehive hair. I stand and watch as she ashes her cigarette and turns her eyes back to the episode of Andy Griffith I had interrupted. The whole place smells like smoke and day-old Hunt Brothers Pizza.

I go to the candy-aisle first and shove a roll of Hubba Bubba bubblegum into my pocket. My palms are sweating when I reach for a Pop-Tart and I knock a mess of Little

I take the blade from her. I can feel her eyes burning holes through the top of my scalp as I drop my head.

Debbie cakes onto the ground. I sweep them under the shelf with my shoe and head towards the drinks.

Cool air from inside the fridge pushes towards me as the door of the refrigerator falls shut. I shove an orange soda under my waistband. The slick aluminum feels like ice on my skin. I'm thinking about grabbing another soda when I hear footsteps coming up behind me. I'm sure as shit I'm about to go to jail. I'm thinking about that headless man creeping up on me when a hand touches my shoulder.

"You dropped this, sugar." It's a woman's voice.

I turn to find the lady from behind the counter standing in front of me. In her hand is the knife Dan gave me. I take the blade from her. I can feel her eyes burning holes through the top of my scalp as I drop my head.

"You better be careful with that, boy," she says. "Wouldn't want you to get hurt."

Out of the corner of my eye, I see her peer down at the shadowed hump at my waistband. She reaches her hand out and lifts up my sweaty T-shirt to reveal the edge of the Pop-Tart wrapper where it peeks out of my pocket. The plastic crinkles against the fabric when she pulls her hand back. She doesn't mention the soda.

I hadn't even noticed that I dropped the blade, but she'd seen it, and she wasn't afraid like Dan said she would be, not in the slightest. I was silly to think she'd be afraid of a nine-year old boy who was sweating bullets and looked like he was bound to shit his britches at the sound of a cough.

"You ain't in trouble," she says. "Just promise me one thing."

I raise my eyes from the linoleum floor. I had been staring at the reflection of a Newport sign that read FIRE IT UP in neon green letters, but the words are backwards, so it takes me a minute to unscramble the letters.

I ask what.

"Don't you ever steal from anywhere but here, you understand? I might let it slide, but not everybody will. You're lucky it wasn't somebody else behind the counter."

I say I promise.

"Now, shoo," she says, "You interrupting my TV program."

She motions me away with her hand and returns to her seat behind the counter. I run out of the door and don't look back.

Dan is nowhere to be found when I get outside. The soda can sits empty right where he left it. I scan the parking lot for him, but he is gone. I can't help but wonder if he'd sent me inside just to get away from me.

I can feel my heartbeat picking up speed now that I know I'm alone. My palms grow sweaty. For a second, I think about going back inside and asking that lady to call my mother, but I decide against it. She'd already done enough for me today, and I know I can't ask her to do such a thing.

I walk across the parking lot and back onto the side of the road. There are no cars, only the sound of a train rumbling in the distance. I look in the direction of Dan's house, and then I look towards my own. Both ways, the road appears long and winding before me. Heat rises off of the asphalt like smoke. I remove the soda from my waistband and chug it as I trek onward through the crude, red mud towards my home. But this time, I don't stop to rest, and I don't cry. The weeds tickle my legs as I move, and I imagine that I am a soldier with a long, black, slender gun resting on my shoulder. And behind me there is a man ready to shoot me down if I falter. ■

SOMEONE SAID ONCE
THAT GOD LIVES ON

the other side of the lake.
It might be so. I've heard
if you gather leaves to set
on fire & breathe the smoke,
God will emerge from behind
a holly tree & answer three questions.

Such as why do I have to burn
things to have a conversation
with Him. Or why I can't seem
to ever find a comfortable pair
of socks. Or why can't I pinch
a raindrop between my thumb
& forefinger to squeeze it & see
the world clearly, only for a moment,
& know what my future holds.

I've never been to the other side
of the lake. The bridge is almost
always out & it's too far to swim.
A man from town once waded out,
his pockets filled with rocks.
His glasses washed up a few days
later & when I put them on,
the view through the cracked lenses
hurt so much I threw them back into
the water where they sank
without so much as a ripple.

Underneath the tree roots God
slinks about as a black snake,
warming Himself in the afternoon
sun & slowly digesting mice. Or
maybe He's a starling, His wings
shimmering from a high branch.
I suppose He watches those who
come to talk, sees their hesitations,
the match trembling in their hands.

MICHAEL PITTARD

CIVIL WAR BATTLEFIELD: CULPEPER, VIRGINIA 2019

There's no one else here.
Only the rusty cutout
silhouettes of riflemen,
fingers waiting to fire.

On the cedar mountain,
radio antennae blink
blue & green lights.
Ticks crawl on every

blade of grass & chest-
high weed & purple flower.
I read that these battles
only matter moment

by moment. A cannon
ball here, an unsheathed
saber there, all
flourishes & folderol.

Some men come here
every August, sleep
together in the thicket,
rush & stab & hold

each other, reenact
hunger, pain, a dying
call. Why have we
come here?

The signage talks
of trampled corn & wheat.
You gather buttercups
& dragonfly husks.

I trace names on all
the headstones, my
fingers steady & true.

MICHAEL PITTARD

SAND FLEA

If I stand here long enough the sand
might blister my feet, sizzle the lines

etched on my soles, burn the broken
pieces of sea oats caught in my toes.

My brother once held a sand flea
in his hands & it burrowed without

end into the crevices of his fingers.
I should move my feet, put on flip-flops,

rush into the saltwater, anything
to stop the quick reddening of my skin.

Out to sea is a freighter, looming
in front of the midday sun. I cannot

understand its size, how it destroys
the fiction of gravity & horizons,

loaded as it is with industrial waste,
ball bearings, or fuzzy bunny slippers.

I could swim out there, if I wanted,
climb up the metal rungs & explain

to the captain how good I am at lifting
with my legs, that yes, I can operate

a ship's crane, & here, let me prove it.
I can sleep in a hammock in a nor'easter.

I'll pick up Mandarin & Farsi, no sweat.
Oh how the great moments in life pass

like this ship on the water, there for all
to see yet moving out to that invisible line

impossibly fast, until they fall off the edge
of the Earth & nothing can catch them.

MICHAEL PITTARD

WHERE DO YOU COME FROM?

RACHEL KESSELMAN

Larksville, Pennsylvania

My grandparents always called it the *parlor*, never the *living room*.

The TV stand was really the empty shell of a 1990s television set inside of which they had placed the flatscreen they were forced to buy when it died. They did not like how thin new televisions were, they had said, and they liked the cabinet that was built in to the old one. Their TV consequently looked like a shadow box theater, and when it was turned on, it seemed you were watching something very far away.

My grandmother's two-foot wedding portrait had been propped on top of it, in front of which was what resembled a white cake box.

"Here she is, Rach," my grandfather said, reaching for the box.

I did not understand what was inside until he put it in my hands, its weight remarkably heavy for its size.

"Don't make no sense!" he said. "I'm older. I was supposed to go first."

"How many times do I have to tell you? It's not always age that makes you go," my mother replied. She turned to me, seeking agreement.

But all I could focus on was the empty couch. It had been over a decade since I had seen it unoccupied, its floral print faded on the seat cushions where my grandmother would lie.

And then, how the scent of *pierogies* and onions was there, even though no one was in the kitchen, as though it were oozing out of the walls.

I placed the box on the coffee table, still sticky with the rings of her teacups.

"Don't make no sense," Grandpa repeated.

■ ■ ■

Paris, one month earlier

The students' exuberance ripped through the stone courtyard of the *lycée* like a tornado, destroying any trace of fatigue or indifference in its ruthless path. Colorful vinyl backpacks swung from their shoulders as they released bursts of laughter into the spring air, their arms dancing in the space before them as though the world were their theater, a place to be explored for expression.

They were invincible in that uniquely American way, their smiles stretching across the entire width of their bright faces.

My French students, overwhelmed by the amount of movement and noise, eventually succumbed to the American students' hugs, smiling over a mixture of bafflement and wonder. The two communicated, side by side, in two extremes: one utterly unobstructed and one of great reserve.

I had spent months preparing for this moment: the coveted French American exchange I had organized after years of teaching in Paris.

But that day, when it was actually happening, I was elsewhere.

■ ■ ■

The past

I was born and raised in my grandmother's kingdom.

A proud Polish Catholic, my grandmother taught my sister and me words like *czekać* and *pierzyna*, though she did not speak Polish fluently. She had a portrait of Jesus in her kitchen, where she would prepare *haluski* and *kielbasa* while we waited for our parents to retrieve us after work. The AM radio on top of the refrigerator would crackle with tunes from an alternate universe, singing soft tales of courtship through the screeching static.

Grandma loved America and told us that everything was safer, more prosperous and just plain better in the 1950s. At her house, we'd travel back in time, and while we were reluctant to admit it, we were fascinated. We'd look through drawers for old relics like paleontologists for fossils: trying to understand how we got here.

As I grew up and left Luzerne County, I was able to locate the difference between where we came from and where we were.

Grandma, however, could not.

Her Luzerne County of glory and abundance simply did not allow for any contradiction. As the world outside continued changing, as generations grew up and left, it became harder for Grandma to preserve her world. She left her house less and less, until finally, when I was in college, she resigned to a life on her living room couch, watching the outside with a pair of binoculars and the only companion that shared her vision: the beer cans tucked behind the cushions.

Grandma chose to live in another time.

After college, I chose to live on another continent.

Where I come from, we're all trying to escape something.

■ ■ ■

Last December

December first was the perfect birthdate for my grandmother.

In rural Pennsylvania, the transition into this month is one of the few life changes that one readily welcomes. Workers relax with a little less guilt, anxiously awaiting a small holiday vacation. Children come to the mall to pose for perfect pictures with Santa, his whimsical snow- laden backdrop hiding the damp, outdated storefronts. There are new faces in church that everyone pretends are regular, and all are hypnotized into a dream-like state under the heavier puffs of incense at Mass.

People flock inside, for the outside world becomes colder and bitter. Here, they create the world they wish they'd lived in, excessively decorating and illuminating, and for a brief moment, they actually believe they have successfully transformed their lives into something completely different.

On this day an ocean away, I left a library to find a city clad in a more conservative amount of décor. A line of pines in front of the Panthéon was strung with blue lights; the boulevards held simple words in uniform colors, *Joyeuses fêtes, Meilleurs voeux*. I decided to walk home and call my grandmother on my way.

Transatlantic conversations with Grandma usually followed the same pattern. She would express enthusiasm for my call until eventually saying she did not want to hold up the line because she knew how expensive long distance was, despite my insisting that I had free calls to the US.

A line of pines in front of the Panthéon was strung with blue lights; the boulevards held simple words in uniform colors, Joyeuses fêtes, Meilleurs voeux.

I managed to tell her about the French-American student exchange I was organizing, just three months away, and she said to make sure to tell them that my grandmother said *bonjour*.

Then, through the strange buzz of her outdated telephone, she broke from script.

"Grandpa and I were just sitting here talking today," she said. "We were saying, Rachel is the farthest away, but we always know we will hear from her. We know we will always hear from Rachel."

I always felt guilty for living in Paris, the place I had dreamed of since adolescence, my literary mecca. The City of Light was overly extravagant for my working-class roots of anthracite and pickup trucks. Every time I'd visit Pennsylvania, my grandparents would ask not if but when I was coming back, as the idea of returning to Europe seemed preposterous to them when they lived in the Best Country in the World.

But on her birthday that year, my grandmother's soft expression of gratitude for my presence in my physical absence lifted a small weight from my shoulders.

Two weeks later, she was admitted to the hospital.

■ ■ ■

The view from the medical center was strangely the most beautiful I had ever seen of my hometown: the Appalachian Mountains rolling indigo in the distance, the lights of the small houses twinkling like stars in the sunset.

Grandma had a form of rare liver cancer, but this diagnosis seemed to be but one small detail. The doctors were more concerned about her overall physical state, as things seemed to continually fail, one after another, like dominos. Eventually, though, she became stable, and even moved from the ICU to a less alarming floor.

Through it all, an uncanny sense of nothingness pervaded. Characteristic of Luzerne County mining people, my family never really spoke of feelings. Standing around her hospital bed, my mother, grandfather and aunt would arrange Grandma's flowers and covers as though they were doing the dishes, talking about the local news over the noise.

My grandmother, however, spoke otherwise.

"I want to go home and die," she would say.

"We'll bring you a plate up for Christmas," they'd reply.

One night, I sat with my grandmother alone with a pile of student exams on my lap, their foreign English more familiar to me than this uncharted territory of hospitals and illness. She was sleeping steadily, and when she suddenly stirred awake, I asked if she wanted something to drink. We were having a hard time getting her to eat—or do anything, really.

But this time, she responded to my question with a nod. I retrieved her protein shake and put the straw to her mouth. She took a few sips, staring off into the distance, until she shook her head to tell me she was finished, her squinting eyes expressing a disgust for the taste.

I put the drink back on the counter near her bed. I asked if she wanted to watch TV, but she didn't respond. I stroked her arm, searching for words in what I knew would be a very brief window of waking.

She turned her head suddenly to look up at me.

"I love you, Rach," she said.

■ ■ ■

A week later, I had to return to Paris for work. Here, every time I called my mother for updates, Grandma seemed to be either the same or improving. For two months, everyone was focused on preparing her return home.

When I called my mother three days into the American exchange students' arrival, she announced my grandmother would be returning home, but not for the reason we had thought.

"There's nothing more they can do," my mother said.

Later that week, my boss asked for an update on the exchange students.

"How is it going with the Americans?" she asked.

Which ones? I thought.

She looked at me, confused, but when I opened my mouth to talk, I began to cry.

At any moment in Paris, France or Larksville, Pennsylvania, Grandma could leave us. The six-hour difference doubled time: noon was also six, nine was three; sometimes night was day and day was night.

The doctors said it varied for each individual person, their *rendez-vous* with death. For Grandma, they said, it could be twelve hours to two days.

My mother would stand on the lawn in front of my grandparents' house to talk to me, the March wind blowing through the phone. She said going outside gave her air. I would imagine her standing there, the site of the Easter egg hunts of my childhood, when Grandma would put quarters in the plastic eggs, Grandpa pieces of coal, and we'd return inside to the palms Grandma had wedged behind the Jesus portrait in the wooden kitchen. I thought of the spring expression she used to say: *in like a lion, out like a lamb.* Scenes of population were the only ones that came to mind: Grandma and Grandpa sitting on the porch, my sister and I studying the creek that ran parallel to the mountain road, my parents lingering in the driveway before their divorce.

Now, my mother alone on the lawn.

At dawn on Saint Patrick's Day, exactly one week after her return, Grandma left.

■ ■ ■

After, words

My mother sent me a picture of a white legal pad covered in her cursive script.

Member of Roman Catholic Church. Adoring
grandmother. Avid sports fan. Preceded in death by.
Survived by. There will be no calling hours.
Could you write the obituary, Rachel?

I remembered talking to fellow English majors in college, their love of words birthed from the books they had devoured as children, from their parents' bedtime stories.

Mine had come from an absence.

I thought of all the times I would be eating breakfast back in Pennsylvania, my family's noses peering over the newspaper: *so-and-so just died, isn't that a shame.*

Grandma's obituary was the most difficult piece of writing I had ever been assigned. An overly embellished text would be inappropriate for the people of Larksville, yet my mother's list of statements read more like a police blotter. Reviewing my mother's text, thinking about my own additions, I realized how much I did not know about my grandmother: how much no one knew about my grandmother.

Such is, perhaps, the natural reaction to a writing of this kind. But my grandmother's seclusion, her choice to live in a reality unshared by the rest of the world, left us all at arm's length, never able to really know what was going on in her life.

Like my mother, I, too, had written a list, one of specific things that I associated with Grandma: Noxzema cold cream, *Bye-Bye Baby Bunting*, the sound of her feet sticking to the linoleum.

I studied it until I found the object with which I might be able to shape the obituary: the hanging baskets on her porch. These flowers were a symbol of her desire to keep certain things alive, her kindest exchange with the outside world.

■ ■ ■

"C'est là, Madame?"

It's here?

My French students marveled at the sprawling American campus: a large, new school building, multiple sports fields of trimmed emerald grass, lines of identical school buses. We had arrived at the high school in the suburbs of Washington, D.C. for our stay in the exchange.

"Bienvenue aux Etats-Unis!" the host teacher exclaimed.

Here, I witnessed the inverse scene of three weeks earlier, as though the negative of a photo: my students' reserve was striking amongst the energetic flurry of the American teenagers. In their natural habitat, the Americans were able to take up even more space, their greetings to each other playful bumps of the shoulder, mocked versions of old-fashioned high fives, enthusiastic fist- pumps and hugs. There was the jingling of keychains and sports zippers and the adjusting of drawstrings. My students stood paralyzed amongst all this movement, appearing like small Old World adults on this wild American frontier.

At the end of the first school day, we were invited to the weekly school assembly in the gym. The entire high school sat in the bleachers watching the portable podium below. Members of various clubs and teams made announcements, giving updates on fundraisers, asking the audience for applause they readily gave. When they announced our visit, I was asked to say a few words.

I took the microphone and looked out at all the eager young faces of America. A sleeping scoreboard hung high on the wall, surrounded by flags of competitions past. I considered for a moment this culture of enthusiasm and excitement, so opposite of what I had been feeling over the previous few weeks.

Long before her seclusion, Grandma would take me to my older sister's elementary school basketball games. I would sit with her in the bleachers, listening to the sound of it all: the sneakers squeaking on the floor, the rattling plastic from the homemade lollipops, the onset of Grandma's cheers. I never understood the game, instead paying expert attention to all the vibrations, following Grandma's lead to yell out in support.

"Nous sommes ravis d'être ici," I said.

We are delighted to be here.

I spoke in French a while, before returning to English. American students approached me with a flurry of questions as they exited, their faces full of unbridled curiosity.

■ ■ ■

Where do you come from?

The drive from Washington, D.C. to Northeastern Pennsylvania took about five hours. I already knew this journey because it was the same I had driven more than once to get a visa at the French consulate: the first leg on a trip to a foreign land.

Work had given me permission to visit my family the weekend our students would be with their host families, my French colleague staying in the area in case of any emergencies. I rented a red compact car, so light and opposite from the SUVs of my rural upbringing that I felt like I was riding some sort of electric bicycle, unstable and feather-like on the five-line highway.

Traffic around the city made for stretches of great immobility, until finally I was released, free to roam, into the no-man's-land of Appalachian Pennsylvania.

I went directly to my grandparents' home, to the parlor.

"Don't make no sense," Grandpa repeated.

We never had a funeral for my grandmother.

"Wait till I go," Grandpa said.

As I write, she is still on top of the shadowbox theater.

That weekend, I discovered my mother's house newly equipped with surveillance equipment: cameras had been attached to her windows and doors. Sitting together in the living room, she showed me the application on her iPad that made separate video files for specified time slots. She searched in its seemingly endless history for the single video that would prove her neighbor really did throw lit cigarette butts under

Traffic around the city made for stretches of great immobility, until finally I was released, free to roam, into the no-man's-land of Appalachian Pennsylvania.

her car. He had attached plastic bags to his house, she said, because when they moved in the wind, they would set off her security alarm.

Shutters had multiplied on her windows, making the entire downstairs dark at any time of day. The decorations on the walls had doubled, too, a mixture of neat colonial portraits and somber impressionist landscapes.

I felt, in her living room, as though in a bunker. The television oscillated from foreground to background in our conversation, my mother's attention bouncing from TV to tablet to me.

"It's Hitchcock," she said, pointing to the well-dressed woman on the screen. "He's planning to kill her."

When my mother left for groceries, I sat on the porch, squinting in the bright outdoor afternoon. There was a cacophony of new spring bird calls, the chill of late March. A freight train sounded in the distance, repeating until it disappeared to a place too far away to remain audible.

When I returned to Washington, my students recounted their weekends of amusement parks and restaurants, the enormous couches in their host families' basements and the unbelievable number of sports everyone played. They were happy to be reunited, unable to visit each other by foot.

"Mais Madame," they said. "Everyone here lives so far away from each other!"

"Distance is measured differently here," I said.

After our museum visits, I took their picture under the cherry blossoms. Clusters of flowers hung above their heads like clouds from a faraway place. ■

THE SPRINGS

I can still feel
      the shaking of your truck bed
cut-black sour of Grizz mint
      & you driving me out into the
night of bruises & smoke shared
      breath-full and the father
buying us bar burgers
      click swift of thighs jagged (yours)
pressed to and held taut (mine)
      song of boys growing dank
twisted love returned in knuckles iron
      protection (you)
& a mouthful of nails pressed hot
      glittering crimson
the bore is crying
      your name—
potato-vodka curled deep gut
      the slide twined unkempt curls
now wet ridden in heat & the
      summer of fire returned
it was your Chevy parked slant
      we sat & watched the blaze
as lovers the drive-in
      boys becoming ———
the ash falling softly
      stuffing our mouths silent

SAGE MARSHALL

MY BROTHER BUYS A COLONY

The female flea begins laying eggs two days after
her first blood meal. She salivates while the
sky-skin warms. She dies six times a year, muddy
with capstar bleach & claw.

My brother holds my head beneath the
pearl-drunk grasses, pressing my nose into
an ant colony.

If I let my eyes unfocus, I can see
fleas jump between the folds of grass.
They flee toward the scar-bright wounds overhead,
looking for a place to burrow.

When I was three I let go of the side of the pool
and sank calmly to the bottom. Mom says
I stared up at their water-eaten faces, unbothered.

Down here, it's always another litter, another host-beast
laying eggs in the wounds. My mouth covers the
sand hives & the larvae in the water,

an open kiss:
new limbs, old food chains
a hand on the back of my neck.

KELSEY DAY

LINE OF SUBARUS AT THE TRAIL OF TEARS STATE PARK: A CALL AND RESPONSE

I cradle the silk-blisters, lick the bed-wounds
but between the heat glares
roots grow into each other,
a rust-eaten pipe kisses along
I see this & want to translate loudly, to
copy & paste the scars on the bark
each view squeezing sap-dough
excellent business model,
the algorithm, like syrup squeezed
I cradle the silk-blisters, lick the bed-wounds

I fasten each lock on the window
a wet cut opens like a palm
tender & suicidal knots
the sheets of spasming mud
lay claim to a sacred pain
with a tortured filter, a corpse-like sheen
from the body
the apocalypse
between the cracks of my teeth.
I sleep without dreaming for days

KELSEY DAY

CRAFTING
FIRST-PERSON NARRATORS:

LESSONS FROM TONI MORRISON'S *A MERCY*

DANIEL KENNEDY

A few weeks ago, one of my creative writing students drafted an autofictional piece about high school friends competing for class office. The piece demonstrated good instincts, but it was overwritten. My student recognized this, too, after we read her work aloud. We agreed kids eating breakfast at an IHOP would likely say "tired" instead of "somnambulant." She asked how an author could write lyrically without overwriting, especially in first person.

I think about this challenge a lot. I grew up in rural Pennsylvania and tend to write about underprivileged rural characters. Can these characters speak with elevated diction and syntax? Are they capable of ascribing figurative language to visceral feelings?

One might encounter these questions in a workshop. While they aren't entirely devoid of merit, they're often framed as reductive binaries. Methods for solving the voice/verisimilitude riddle differ, depending on the work and its author.

I wasn't sure this response would be useful to my student. I wanted to equip her with craft strategies—not bog her down with rigid rules. Fortunately, literature contains great examples of first-person narrators who are almost preternaturally articulate and believable. Florens, the protagonist of Toni Morrison's *A Mercy*, is one such narrator.

A Mercy is set in the 1680s. Florens is a Black, teenage enslaved person. She spent her early years on a Maryland plantation before she was sold, at her mother's behest, to Jacob Vaark, an ambitious Dutch farmer. Given the oppressive circumstances in which she lives, Florens would probably not possess Morrison's linguistic skill; and yet, her poetic capability is established on page one: "You can think what I tell you a confession, if you like, but one full of curiosities familiar only in dreams and during those moments when a dog's profile plays in the steam of a kettle."

Morrison fearlessly occupies Florens's perspective. She turns constraint into possibility, a craft technique that echoes Florens's personal growth as she wrestles with her life's many constraints. Over the course of the novel, we come to understand Florens's lyricism is true to her character's experience and plausible. How does Morrison strike this exquisite balance?

1. The Strategic Release of Background Information

A Mercy is a challenging read. It contains various points of view and moves back and forth through time. In the first chapter, we learn Florens' sections of the book are written texts: "Confession we tell not write as I am doing now." Her epistolary narrative addresses her mother and the man she loves, a mysterious blacksmith. At the same time, her sections describe much of the novel's central plot.

The blacksmith, a free, Black man, arrives among a troupe of laborers to build a mansion for the Vaarks. He and Florens engage in a romance shortly thereafter. She's devasted when he leaves without saying goodbye; the sense of abandonment reminds her of her mother. Vaark dies from smallpox just as his dream home is completed. On the day of his funeral, his wife, Rebekka, realizes she is sick as well. She sends Florens to fetch the blacksmith, who, during his tenure with the Vaarks, healed an enslaved person named Sorrow. The book concludes with the first-person voice of Florens's mother. She addresses Florens, explaining she sent her daughter away to protect her. Florens remains tragically unaware of her mother's motive.

The novel's choral narration operates like a set of mirrors. The structure allows Morrison to organically incorporate details of Florens's educational background. Lina, a Native American woman (her tribe is unnamed), lives on the Vaark farm. She becomes Florens's surrogate mother. From Lina, we gather that "[Florens] learned quickly, was eager to know more." Rebekka believes Florens will be successful in her journey to the blacksmith—a journey on which their lives depend—"because [Florens] was clever."

Florens's life stems from the horrific abuse her mother endured on the D'Ortega plantation. In the final chapter, her mother notes how a reverend taught her and Florens "letters" on the plantation. She knows there is "magic in learning." By equipping Florens with a desire for knowledge and getting her away from the D'Ortegas, she gives her daughter a glimmer of hope for a safer life.

Nonetheless, Florens needs to understand why her mother gave her up and why the blacksmith left her. This need comprises the emotional core of her desire to learn. Morrison elegantly braids necessary exposition with resonant emotional themes. In doing so, she reinforces the plausibility of Florens's skills with language.

2. Grammatical Experimentation

Florens's dialect represents a particular upbringing and set of experiences. The tight weave of awkward grammar and eloquent description shapes her voice. She frequently conflates verbs with nouns. At one point, she says, "I hide from everything of creep and slouch." In context, "creep" and "slouch" are verbs, but in this sentence, they're used as objects of a preposition. She employs lyrical run-on sentences: "Night is thick no stars anyplace but sudden the moon moves." Adjectives and adverbs are swapped: "She sudden sits."

Morrison's syntax often corresponds with the rhythm of a scene, but the technical architecture is veiled by poignant grammatical distortions. Florens reports, "The argue is done and Mistress drives us away. After a while she pulls the horse to a stop. She turns to Sorrow and slaps her face more, saying fool. I am shock. Mistress never strikes us." Here, the sentences shorten, reflecting Florens's surprise. The swapping of a noun for a verb ("shock") is arresting on a syntactic level, allowing the form and content to merge in a way that elevates the language. Morrison utilizes this technique throughout Florens' chapters. Another: "Sudden a sheet of sparrows falls from the sky and settle in the trees." The misused adjective and disagreement in number ("sheet" and "settle") allows the lyricism to dip and soar, like the sparrows, like Florens's hopes for a better future.

Even when misuse and lyricism are not braided in a single sentence, they tend to be situated in proximity, maintaining the nuanced beauty of Florens's voice: "Where they once are is nothing. Only apple trees aching to bud and an echo of laughing boys." The inconsistent verb tense is followed by a striking image. Moreover, the image is layered with subtext. Like the boys and the trees, Florens yearns for the opportunity to blossom.

3. Imagistic Network

Morrison generates a precise imagistic network, bolstering the credibility of Florens's descriptions. When describing what she sees, Florens uses the imagery available to her: that of the home, the farm, and nature. She says of the blacksmith, "What I know is that I wilt when you go and am straight when mistress sends me to you." Describing a spring snowfall, Florens writes, "We are nervous also but we sit still as the flakes come down and stick to our shawls and hats, sugaring our eyelashes and flouring the men's wooly beards. Two women face into the wind that whips their hair like corn tassel, their eyes slits of shine." Her figurative language springs naturally from her life's points of reference.

Occasionally, antecedents fall on the same page as their figurative implementations. Florens climbs a hill covered in "scarlet flowers." Further down the page, she notes that Vaark is "rosy with scrubbing" after a bath. She employs synesthesia—perhaps unintentional for Florens, though certainly intentional for Morrison: "The creaking wheel and rushing water are what shape the quiet."

Before Florens sets out to fetch the blacksmith, Rebekka gives her a letter. It's meant to assure her safe passage.

Florens stumbles upon a Puritan farmstead. A paranoid man confiscates the letter. He says he must examine it to discern if Florens is a demon. She sneaks off, resuming her journey, but now, she sees the missing letter manifested in the landscape: "The sun empties itself, pouring what is left through tree shadow." She uses animal metaphors to express her vulnerability, too: "Without [the letter] I am a weak calf abandon by the herd, a turtle without shell." The metaphors are appropriate for the situation, and they resonate on a macro-thematic level.

4. Intensity of Emotion

Florens's emotional states trigger or halt her lyrical flourishes. When she feels impassioned, her language elevates. In moments of defeat or ennui, she resorts to simple diction and terse syntax.

When Florens finally reaches the blacksmith, she discovers he's looking after an orphan named Malaik. She writes, "I worry as the boy steps closer to you...As if he is your future. Not me." Upon hearing of Rebekka's dire condition, the blacksmith immediately departs, leaving Malaik with Florens. Her focus drifts from Malaik to the blacksmith on the next page. Again, her language heightens: "I take off Sir's boots and lie on your cot trying to catch the fire smell of you. Slices of starlight cut through the shutters." The description is packed with sensory detail.

While the blacksmith is away, Florens grows resentful of Malaik. The boy fears her and cries persistently. She explains, "I am trying to stop him not hurt him. That is why I pull his arm. To make him stop. Stop it." Florens doesn't attempt to artfully depict her impatience. The blacksmith arrives just as she accidentally breaks the boy's arm. The blacksmith knocks her to the ground, calls her "slave," and tells her to leave.

Curled on the floor, she sees the blacksmith "take [Malaik] to lie down with the doll and return to [her] [his] broken face, eyes without glee, rope pumps in [his] neck." In this sentence, Florens's language seesaws on the conjunction, which separates an emphasis on Malaik and an emphasis on the blacksmith. The first half of the sentence is simple and direct, while the second half is vivid and lyrical.

5. Story & The Writing Process

Florens is a retrospective narrator. She draws upon her experiences, the "memorable nights" when she would "[listen] in rigid delight to Lina's stories," and her educational training to construct her own story, making its shapeliness more digestible to the critical reader. Additionally, Florens's motivation to write appears in the first chapter: "From the day you disappear I dream and plot. To learn where you are and how to be there." Within the novel, the writing process is configured as a realm of possibility, a space of escape and connection. Florens's text has a rhetorical quality as well. It attempts to persuade a specific audience—the blacksmith, and, on a subtler, more symbolic level, her mother—to see the story's events from her perspective. The complexity of Florens's myriad motivations to write evocatively is inseparable from the depth of her character.

The opening chapter ends with Florens arguing she knows "how their eyes go when they choose. How they raise them to look at me hard, saying something I cannot hear. Saying something to me, but holding the little boy's hand." She's describing a distant memory of her mother holding her little brother's hand as D'Ortega and Vaark conduct their business; she's simultaneously describing the blacksmith and Malaik. Her synthesized audience mirrors her language, which rarely operates on a single level.

At one point, Florens "dreams a dream that dreams back at [her]." In it, she's horrified when no reflection appears in a brilliant blue lake. Her sense of self-worth is imperiled throughout the novel. Writing redeems her. In her final chapter, she remembers the blacksmith is illiterate. He won't be able to read her story, which is etched all over the room she occupies. She considers how he may one day learn. Even if he doesn't, her "careful words, closed up and wide open, will talk to themselves."

Florens's story is a recursive dream that molds limitation into a unique form of expression. Despite the enduring difficulty of her life, she recognizes the meaning and worth of her voice. Her new understanding connects her to her mother's long-ago hope—that an unimaginably painful decision would result in a better future for Florens.

■ ■ ■

Towards the end of my student's scene, the narrator implies a crush on another character, noting how she "shot him a million-watt smile." He fails to notice. The scene concludes with a curt final sentence: "We ate and dipped." The sentence parallels the narrator's disappointment. "Dipped"— an expertly chosen verb—captures the voice of a high schooler and, metaphorically, portrays her heartache.

It is folly to assume a prescribed set of rules can accommodate the nuances of narrative voice. Instead, we can turn to our best literature for craft strategies. Florens reminds us that first-person narrators can be colloquial and evocative. More importantly, she reminds us why we turn to fiction in the first place: it is a landscape "full of curiosities familiar only in dreams." ■

THE IDEA OF ANCESTORS

After Ethredge Knight

My father bobs down the river of ancestors,
drifts in darkness where our lights dot the shore.

In the sky white pocket handkerchiefs lie crumpled;
white tank trucks and barges, white tank cars
roll from a chemical plant on high. Below,
the river carries his lifetime of shoveled dirt,
his black coffee, unfiltered cigarettes.

My father knows I disdain him and all his people.
I am none of them. They are none of me.
He knows the river is dark and cold and dirty.
He knows the little he has always had to offer.

Oh my yellow-eyed father, yellow-eyed as I am,
when I enter the water, I will not be denied.

SUE CHURCHILL

AND I AM NEXT OF KIN

After Samuel Taylor Coleridge

Gotta be bad karma—
them, on the job, the road
without shoulders—them,
straddling the entrails, setting to.

Not so bad, maybe
if I'd done it on purpose,
but I veered, went wide.
The bird did, too.

A big black vulture
had shown up in my poem
that very morning—
what message was I receiving

as the bird popped off
my right front headlight,
flopped into the ditch?
Some albatross for my neck.

Some new albatross.
Some noose waiting.

What had I done, pulling these birds,
                 a something in the sky, into my poem-path?

Same stretch of road,
another weary day,
my weary, wary eye.
I top the ridge at fifty:

on my left a house, on my right
two kids at a mailbox:
sister, little brother.
They watch, they know, they wait—

her hand a caution at his chest,
his arms clasped round a . . .
package? backpack? A heavy bulge.
To get past, I accelerate,

but as I pull even,
it tears loose, flings
itself—a cat—I brake.
I swerve. My eyes shut

with dread, but I see the boy's
eyes seeing—the boy,
the boy . . . the boy
does   not   bolt.

The car shudders forward.
The cat, big-shouldered
as if winged, bounds
beyond, and is on the other

side, and I am on
the other side. We are all
on the other side of the thing
that did not happen.

SUE CHURCHILL

BOOK REVIEWS

Jessie van Eerden. *Call It Horses*. Ann Arbor, Mich.: Dzanc Books, 2021. 246 pages. Hardcover. $26.95.

Reviewed by Jayne Moore Waldrop

In *Call It Horses*, three women—a niece, her aunt, an unwanted stowaway—hit the road in a long, rusted Oldsmobile Royale in the late 1980s, leaving Caudell, West Virginia, for Abiquiu, New Mexico, and the desert landscape of Georgia O'Keeffe. From the start, nothing about the trip hints at pleasure or relaxation. Instead, the journey is more of an escape from everything they know as they attempt to outrun the grief and troubles chasing each of them. There's been no planning for the trip, which heightens the atmosphere of escape.

Frankie, the driver and narrator, is in her mid-thirties. She was orphaned as a teenager and raised, sort of, by her aunt Mave. After dropping out of high school, Frankie was homeschooled, sort of, by Mave, who unevenly tried to show Frankie a bigger view of the world through books. As the journey begins, Mave is close to the end of her life from cancer, her condition so fragile she requires portable oxygen tanks and an assortment of pills for the pain. Mave wants to reach Abiquiu, but she can't make it there alone. Nan is a young artist with a black eye courtesy of her husband Dillon, who was Frankie's first love. Nan is unwanted and relegated to the back seat, invited because she has the only car that's still running at the time of departure. She's described as loose in her actions and her words, a revealing indictment in a story built upon the value of language and finding the proper words to name things.

As in the archetypal American road trip, the women head west, traveling through West Virginia, Kentucky, Tennessee, and along I-40 into the desert, in search of the landscape of Georgia O'Keeffe. In sections set at home, the reader can almost feel the heaviness of the lush, humid landscape, a place of forests, caves, and bogs filled with decaying vegetation. There's stark contrast between the thick air that constricts Frankie's airways and the clear, bright paintings of O'Keeffe's desert world filled with flowers and bleached skulls, which are seen as "souvenirs of death."

The novel is structured as a series of letters written by Frankie to Ruth, a deceased linguist who was Mave's longtime lover. Ruth, who had studied the languages and hieroglyphs of the Sinai Desert on sabbaticals, had been Frankie's pen pal for three years when Frankie was a teenager. At the time, Mave and Ruth lived together on the east coast in a relationship considered immoral by Mave's sisters. Ruth, who had grown up with privilege and opportunity, had observed promise in young Frankie's writing, and from that point, both Ruth and Mave encouraged her writing.

Although Frankie and Ruth never meet, their correspondence becomes a private, sustaining lifeline for Frankie during adolescence. After Ruth's death, the letters stop. Mave had returned to West Virginia with an unexpected inheritance of money and books, along with a grief that alcohol couldn't assuage. But even after death, Ruth provides a measure of stability for Frankie amid the cluttered chaos of Mave's life.

The letters provide structure for the novel, but the narrative is remarkably nonsequential, written with layers that need to be peeled like an onion from Frankie's garden. It's a short novel, but not a fast read. Significant details from the past weave throughout the letters. Some readers may wish for more straightforward linear movement in the storytelling.

Frankie's writing finally, carefully, takes shape in the form of a journal documenting the road trip, written on a Dollar Store notepad.

> *I write you about the dead. I write you to stay alive and, after all this time, I write you, still to become myself.... On a rough-lumber table with a vinyl tablecloth, I write this to you. Dear, Ruth, can you feel the unfolding of our disaster? I should write each word as carefully and detailed as a hieroglyph. I should choose sensibly what bird to mean soul, what horse to mean I'm falling fast through time. Each word precious. You taught me that, in the letters you wrote me from your desk in Northampton,*

which I always pictured as dark wood, wide,
strewn with books and, at the corner, a vase
of tulips. What promise did you see in me?
Anyway, I do think it's something else—after the
words, that might be precious. Once language
slips through the sieve, maybe something
remains. Maybe a heart beating.

West Virginia native Jessie van Eerden is the award-winning author of both works of fiction and nonfiction. *Call It Horses*, winner of the Dzanc Fiction Prize, demonstrates creativity as well as precision in research to accurately depict time and place. Her past work includes *The Long Weeping* (Orison Books 2017), named *Foreword* INDIES Book of the Year Award for essay; her debut novel, *Glorybound* (WordFarm), winner of the 2012 *Foreword* Review Editor's Choice Fiction Prize; and the novel *My Radio Radio* (Vandalia Press 2016). Van Eerden teaches creative writing at Hollins University.

The most striking characteristic of the novel is the beauty and precision of its language. The story unfolds through rich, immense vocabulary. Mave tells Frankie that "[a] word is a living thing," which sends Frankie in search of her late mother's Bible with its cover proclaiming it to be The Living Word. Frankie's search doesn't end there. Her pursuit of the right words to put on the page—to make sense of things, to find truth—is a theme that springs organically from a writer who clearly believes in the power of language. ∎

**Kim Michele Richardson. *The Book Woman's Daughter.*
Naperville, Ill.: Mercer University Press, 2022. 352 pages.
Hardover. $26.99.**

Reviewed by Donna M. Crow

For readers who loved Kim
Michelle Richardson's *The Book
Woman of Troublesome Creek,*
this sequel offers another visit to
the hills of Eastern Kentucky, only
one generation after the WPA
implemented the Packhorse Librarian
Project. Yet, *The Book Woman's
Daughter* stands alone as a simple,
sweet story layered with the dark,
complicated issues which still haunt
Appalachia today.

One hundred years after the first large public library was
erected in Boston, while library buildings were popping up
all over the country, in 1952 Appalachia, books were still
carried on horseback across narrow footpaths into hollers,
up hillsides, and along high ridges. The lack of infrastructure
in difficult terrain has kept the descendants of early settlers
regionally isolated, causing Appalachia to be one of the last
places in America to obtain modern living standards. In this
fictionalized but true Appalachian tale, many struggle for
literacy and yearn for news of the outside world, while others
fearfully hang on to the only lives they've known. These
livelihoods are filled with family values, hardscrabble survival,
loyal friendships, and desire for education, yet rife with the
racism, miscegenation laws, and misogyny that plague the
systems of patriarchy and white supremacy.

In *The Book Woman's Daughter,* Richardson balances these juxtaposed ideals by challenging stereotypes, utilizing strong female characters, and forging unlikely friendships. The narrator's infectious love of books, the expansion of literacy, the empowerment of women, and the desire for equality, freedom and justice are the emergent themes. "'Freedom. The word rattled my thoughts. I was relieved there might be a chance of getting it without marrying,'" says our protagonist. "'I was grateful…, but even more appreciative for the librarian work. A job and money—and the books—meant I could at least survive, and do it on my own'". Her literary identity provides Honey with a freedom she struggles to find in her everyday life.

The novel is set in the early fifties and told through the eyes of Honey Lovett, the child Cussy Mary Lovett adopted in the first novel. Readers will remember that Cussy built her reputation among hill-folk as a "bookwoman" who served as part of the Packhorse Librarian Project and provided valuable access to books for her people. Both women carry a genetic trait that causes the blood disorder methemoglobinemia, which tints the skin blue. Both women also have an insatiable appetite for "book-learning" and prove that books are transformative.

Months after reading *The Book Woman's Daughter,* like *The Book Woman of Troublesome Creek,* what sticks are the characters. These characters include the mountain bootlegger who is a compassionate advocate for women's rights and the female social worker who seems hell-bent on sending a minor to jail mainly because of her skin color.

The opening scene sets the stage of trouble for Honey as her parents are whisked away to jail for the legal infraction of having a mixed-race marriage. Being underage and of blue tint herself puts Honey at risk for incarceration as well, so she must stay hidden while she struggles for emancipation. As she embarks on her freedom journey, she comes across a young woman who is just arriving for her new job as the first woman fire-tower watcher in the region. "Being different here in white or black Kentucky puts you on the lowest rung," Honey explains to her new friend. "'[I]t's not against the law to be a minor,'" her friend replies. "'Shouldn't be against the law to love someone either,' says Honey, 'But it sure ought to be against the law for men to decide who you can and can't love'". The two young women become a formidable force against discrimination over the course of the novel.

To some, the book may come across as not being "male-friendly," but upon deeper analysis, there are as many female oppressors as there are male and as many male advocates of freedom and justice as there are female. The narrator's real fight is with an oppressive idealism. This provides credence to the book's criticism of the systems of patriarchy and white supremacy, especially as it rules over the Appalachian region.

For new visitors to these parts, this novel will stand alone as a testament to history, while allowing the reader to dip their toes into the muddy waters of Troublesome Creek and the backwoods trails that are both brutal and beautiful. ■

CROSSHAIRS

I buy my father a Father's Day card
with a deer on the front, its fur gold-embossed

like a struck coin. After I lie on the inside,
I hesitate. Should I tell him how I feel

and ruin his day? *Hi Dad, thanks for teaching me
how not to be a father. Hope you have a nice day*

without me. Before I put the card in the envelope,
I draw a crosshair on the front shoulder

of the deer with a permanent marker.
I only know how to relate to my father

through death. He taught me to aim
for the shoulder—it will go through the heart,

then the lungs if you're at the right angle,
each shoulder blade breaking under

the impact. The deer will be easy to track.
If the card designer meant for that deer

to represent the strength and beauty of all
fathers, then I am killing my own father

in front of him. So be it. He won't understand
the crosshairs as a choice to use the symbols

he gave me against him, the barrel
of my pen hot in my hand. When my father

opens the card and sees I haven't forgotten
the lessons of death he taught me, he will smile.

WILLIAM FARGASON

SONNET WITH BARE BRANCHES

Lord I don't   Lord after I go
I don't want to be remembered
as unkind   as unable to hold
the door for my neighbor Lord

when the fruits of the spirit
are the signs of you   how do I forgive
myself of myself   how Lord do I
when each season a new species

in my body goes extinct   Lord
how do I extend like a green leaf
fighting winter with its greenness
Lord how do I stay   kind toward

the sky   when the only voice I hear
is the one that echoes back

WILLIAM FARGASON

ARS POETICA

I kept my mouth
closed for many years.
I listened to the wind
play the dark branches

like a cello. The rain
in the street had gathered
into a pool I could see
myself in. My hands

left my pockets and joined the air
as if receiving an offering
from a priest in the dirt. I kept
my mouth closed

for many years, and then,
I opened it.

WILLIAM FARGASON

CONTRIBUTORS

Skylar Bensheimer is a writer and former student assistant for *Appalachian Review*. He graduated from Berea College in 2022 with a B.A. in English and a minor in Creative Writing.

A former teacher, **Sue Churchill** currently works in farming, managing a farm and raising a flock of sheep in Woodford County, Kentucky. She grew up in Breckinridge County, and her work is strongly influenced by the rural setting of her life, past and present.

Leo Coffey is a writer born and raised in Western North Carolina. His work engages with class distinctions, gender identity, the tension between memory and reality, and the beauty of forgotten life. He earned his BA in Creative Writing from the University of North Carolina-Asheville. His work has appeared in *Hawaii Pacific Review, Headwaters,* and elsewhere. He currently lives in Knoxville, Tennessee, where he works as a bookseller at Union Ave Books.

Donna M. Crow, a resident of Estill County, Kentucky, is the third generation to live on her family farm. She writes fiction, creative nonfiction, and poetry. Her work has appeared previously in *Appalachian Review, Still: The Journal, Now and Then, The Minnetonka Review, The Louisville Review, Blue Lyra Review,* and others. She received her MFA in Creative Nonfiction from Spalding University.

Kelsey Day is a poet and fiction writer from southern Appalachia. They are the author of two poetry collections, *The Last Four Years* and *Rootlines*. You can read more of their writing at www.kelseydays.com, on Twitter @kelseydaywrites, and on Instagram @kelseydays.

Kathleen Driskell is the Chair of Spalding University's School of Creative and Professional Writing, home of the nationally distinguished low-residency MFA in Writing Program in Louisville, Kentucky. She's the author of the poetry collections *Blue Etiquette: Poems*, a finalist for the Weatherford Award; *Next Door to the Dead*, a Kentucky Voices selection by the University Press of Kentucky and winner of the 2018 Judy Gaines Young Book Award; *Seed Across Snow,* a Poetry Foundation national bestseller; *Laughing Sickness,* and *Peck and Pock: A Graphic Poem.*

William Fargason is the author of *Love Song to the Demon-Possessed Pigs of Gadara* (University of Iowa Press, 2020), winner of the 2019 Iowa Poetry Prize and the 2020 Florida Book Award in Poetry (Gold Medal). His poetry has appeared in *The Threepenny Review, New England Review, Barrow Street, Prairie Schooner, Poetry Northwest, The Cincinnati Review, Narrative,* and elsewhere. He earned an MFA in Poetry from the University of Maryland and a PhD in Poetry from Florida State University. He lives with himself in Sparks Glencoe, Maryland, where he serves as the poetry editor at *Split Lip Magazine.*

Makayla Gay hails from Southeastern Kentucky. She received a BFA in Creative Writing and Philosophy from Converse College in South Carolina. Gay is a current MFA candidate in poetry at Sarah Lawrence College. Gay's work has appeared in *South Carolina Radio, Western North Carolina Magazine, Still: The Journal, CHOMP!, Angles,* and *Red Coyote.*

Daniel Kennedy grew up in rural Pennsylvania. He holds an MFA from Virginia Tech, where he won the Emily Morrison Prize in Fiction. His writing has appeared in *New England Review, The Carolina Quarterly, Arts & Letters, The Madison Review, BULL, Ghost Parachute,* and elsewhere. His work has been nominated for the Pushcart Prize and was awarded the 2022 Inprint Donald Barthelme Prize in Nonfiction. He's currently a PhD candidate in the University of Houston's Creative Writing Program.

Born and raised in the Anthracite Coal Region of Northeastern Pennsylvania, **Rachel Kesselman** now makes her home in Paris. Her writing has received numerous awards including been awarded the Carlisle Family Scholarship for the Squaw Valley Community of Writers Workshop and the Mathey Family Scholarship for the Mendocino Coast Writers' Conference. One of her essays was recently a finalist in *North American Review*'s Terry Tempest Williams Prize. She holds a B.A. in French and English from Bryn Mawr College and a Master's in Comparative Literature and Education from the Sorbonne. She serves as Workshop Director at La Muse Writers and Artists Retreat in the South of France.

Bill King grew up in the Blue Ridge Mountains. He is the 2021 HeartWood Poetry Prize winner and a Pushcart Prize nominee. His work has appeared in *Kestrel, Appalachian Review, 100 Word Story, Still: The Journal, Naugatuck River Review,* and many other journals and anthologies. He holds an M.A. in Creative Writing and a Ph.D. in Literature from the University of Georgia and teaches creative writing and literature at Davis & Elkins College in Elkins, West Virginia. His first chapbook of poetry is *The Letting Go.*

Sage Marshall is a poet, writer, and journalist from southwest Colorado. His poems have been featured in *Arc Poetry Magazine, Emerge Literary Journal, Reverberations Mag,* and elsewhere. He is currently working on a memoir titled *The Barbs.*

Quincy Gray McMichael stewards Vernal Vibe Rise, creates permaculture designs for curious clients, and paints. Her writing—both creative nonfiction and poetry—has been published in *Yes! Magazine, The Dewdrop, Open: A Journal of Arts and Letters, Greenbrier Valley Quarterly,* and is forthcoming from Assay, among other publications. Quincy holds an MFA in Creative Nonfiction from the Naslund-Mann Graduate School of Writing at Spalding University. She is a contributing editor at *Good River Review* and is completing a hybrid memoir that explores obsession and overwork through a blend of poetry and prose.

Kasia Merrill is a fiction writer based in Appalachian Maryland. She holds an MFA in creative writing and works as a publishing director for a children's publishing house. Her fiction has appeared in *Breadcrumbs Mag* and *Fiction International,* and in 2022, she was selected to be a Peter Taylor fellow for the Kenyon Writer's Workshop. She is currently at work on her first novel.

Michael Pittard is an English lecturer at the University of North Carolina at Greensboro. He currently serves as the Book Recommendations editor for *The Bookends Review.* He has an MFA in Poetry from UNCG and is a former poetry editor of *The Greensboro Review.* His poetry has appeared in such places as *Poetry South, Coffin Bell,* and *The Citron Review.*

Jayne Moore Waldrop is the author of *Retracing My Steps, Pandemic Lent: A Season in Poetry* (both from Finishing Line Press), and *Drowned Town* (University Press of Kentucky 2021). *A Journey in Color: The Art of Ellis Wilson,* a picture book biography for young readers, is forthcoming from Shadelandhouse Modern Press. She lives in Lexington, Kentucky.

www.ingramcontent.com/pod-product-compliance
Lightning Source LLC
Chambersburg PA
CBHW070603180626
46817CB00005B/1970